Applause

Before reading "The Italian Dance Quest," I figured I would deepen my understanding of my Italian heritage as well as learn about the intricacies and nuances of the dance world…and I did. I most certainly did. But what I didn't expect is this would be one of those books I keep beside my nightstand, to refer to over and over again. Not only is Anna's visual description of everything she encountered as a dancer, coach, molder of young minds and souls so vivid and authentic, but she connected everything she encountered and learned into life lessons for ANYONE, for all of us.

—Dean Skinner, Author, Visual artist, Cleveland, Ohio

In The Italian Dance Quest, Anna's sensitivity to and keen observations of Italy's cultural differences offer not only a keen and truthful key to interpret the dances covered in the book but also a profound "spaccato" of Anna's personal and professional life from her vision to the reality of becoming the expert on Italian Folk Dances of today.

—Viviana Altieri, Founder and Executive Director, ISTITUTO MONDO ITALIANO, Pittsburgh, PA

A wonderful amalgamation of dance, history, and culture seen through an artist's imagination and the manifested choreographic process took me back to the streets of Italy where inspiration and wonder are not in short supply. The celebration of dance deeply rooted in the Italian experience reminded me of Salieri's Opera "The Stolen Bucket" where two Italian cities actually went to war over a stolen bucket. Passion and drama at its finest. I highly recommend this read.

—Jim Bunting, Director of Jim Bunting Dance Company, Philadelphia, PA

Anna's passion for preservation is necessary and this book showcases just that. As a Professor of Dance, I was impressed with how "The Italian Dance Quest," contained a great detail of the dances shared. This book takes you into a world full of movement and creativity, where authentic Italian dance and family stories bring the heritage to life. Anna's enthusiasm and positive outlook are reflected through each chapter. This enriching dive into Italian dance culture is inspiring and a joy to read.

—Joe Nickel, Dance Professor, Seton Hill University and Owner of Thrive Dance Experience, Pittsburgh, PA

THE ITALIAN DANCE QUEST

Finding Power, Wealth, and Innovation

ANNA HARSH

To maintain the anonymity of the individuals involved, I have changed some details. These are my memories, from my perspective, and I have tried to represent events as faithfully as possible. Any products or companies mentioned in this book are offered as a resource and are not intended in any way to be or to imply as an endorsement of their products or services.

For more information, address: annaharsh.com.
First paperback edition March 2022

Book design by: Anna Harsh
Edited by: N.N. Light Editing Services
Photography by: Greg Harsh, Anna Harsh

Printed by: Tambourine Chronicles in the USA.
TambourineChronicles@gmail.com

ISBN 979-8-9853559-2-5 (paperback)
ISBN 979-8-9853559-3-2 (ebook)

Published by: Tambourine Chronicles
TambourineChronicles@gmail.com

Dedicated to

You, the reader, who loves dance, traditions, preserving heritage, and memories that spark stories of family and friends.

Contents

Preface

This book is an inside look into Italian culture through my quest to preserve Italian dances. I share explorations of culture, music, dance, and traditions that would take anyone years to accumulate on their own. The best way to experience and truly understand the essence of these traditional dances is to gather as much information about the life and history that surrounds the cities that the dances are from, along with the people that perform them. My hope is that you, the reader, will step into a time of wealth, royalty and innovation in the northern regions of Italy. Family legacies are revealed and preserved through the arts, where their passions speak with every paint stroke or gesture in a dance. I believe the art of creating is embedded into the soul of every Italian, and quite possibly every human. Culture, cuisine, and choreography are explored and discussed along with life lessons I learned along the way, all with the ultimate goal to preserve the dances originating in the northern regions of Italy.

This book will help you unlock a few doors uncovering the mystery, beauty, and elegance of the rich culture of the Italian regions. Through these journeys, the reader will discover the lessons learned while traveling and compare and contrast different aspects of each visit. Various folk dances I've mastered are described that originate from different regions in northern Italy. Every city described in this book is north of Rome. Northern Italy and southern Italy have vastly different cuisines, climates and histories. So, it stands to reason their folk dances would have stark contrasts as well. The dances of northern Italy feature upright postures and precise steps and timing. Southern Italian folk dances have earthy, more grounded movements and generally are spontaneous and respond to how a partner is dancing. Join me to explore how the traditions and history of northern Italy are reflected within their folk dances where power, beauty, and innovation are found.

All of my adventures to Italy are continuously filled with surprises, splendor and a bit of risk. Italy is a country where my history began, my present lives, and my future awaits. My mission is to research antiquity, appreciate the culture, preserve the traditions and share the dances that shed light on the heritage I adore. Traveling over the years, I share many thrilling and life-changing events that have occurred. Venturing out of my own backyard gave me a perspective on the world and a chance to view life from many angles. With this book, you will venture with me through various stages of my life: as a child, as a young leader, and married with my husband on an expedition of discovery to five cities in northern Italy. Answer the series of questions at the end of every chapter, titled 5, 6, 7, 8, a phrase used for dancers to start together. I hope it will enhance your experience, allow you to reflect on your life and lead you to find answers.

Finally, I will immerse you in a dancer's perspective of five dances that reflect the regions I visited. The reader will gain insight to choreography techniques used that were influenced by Italian architecture and transportation. I offer various ways to preserve and enjoy physical history so that the next generation can enjoy them in the future.

Introduction

For the past thirty years, I have procured, preserved and performed traditional Italian dances. When traveling, I make it a point to explore new places, veer off the usual paths and experience what it is like to be a true local. Yes, I visited the main piazza and took that gondola ride, but I also observed crafts being made and watched performances to understand what the region had to offer. I gained a greater admiration and understanding from speaking with the locals and asking about their professions and passions. These conversations created a larger picture of what the traditional dances I have been studying should look like and insight into life in different time periods. Taking these explorations as a child gave me a greater comprehension of the definition of culture, traditions and how I fit into this big world.

Experiencing another person's culture helps build empathy and deepens perceptions. Learning this idea at an early age sets up a child for success in life, no matter what profession they choose. My wish is for everyone to explore different cultures by learning a new language, tasting a new spice or dancing a different style. It can be inspiring and transformative. It opens the mind up to new ideas, a better appreciation of others and allows the conclusion that there is always more to learn in life.

I've taken numerous trips to Italy, but three are prominently featured in this book. I grew up straddling two worlds: being an Italian and an American. All four of my grandparents were born in southern Italy and immigrated in the early 1920s. My parents were born in the United States of America. I have two older siblings, my sister Diana and my older brother Stephen. When I was twelve, my mom, my older brother, who was nineteen years old at the time, and I embarked on our first trip to Italy. We visited Milan, Florence, Venice, Rome and met our cousins for the first time in Calabria. This adventure was life-changing in so many ways. As a wide-eyed preteen, I soaked up as much culture and history as possible, meeting flesh and blood relatives bringing me closer physically to this idea of being Italian that I have grown up with only through stories as a child. My vision board in sixth grade was filled with photos of Italy and meeting family. This vision board creation was about to become a reality.

My mom at this time has just turned fifty. We traveled a couple of years after both her parents had passed away in the mid-1980s. After exchanging emotional letters and phone calls to relatives in Italy, we were finally meeting her father's brother, my great uncle, and his family for the first time. This was life altering for all of us, especially my mom. She knew this would be her only journey to Italy and was determined to make the most of it for herself, and us. It would be twenty-five more years before I could return to visit Calabria and see them again as an adult.

The second excursion I re-encounter is with dancers. About six years after founding my own touring dance company, Allegro Dance Company, I organized a performance tour with a select group of company members. We were traveling to Italy to tour, perform traditional and modern dances, and soak up the culture. We explored Rome, Venice, Florence, and Montecatini. Leading a group through another country and preparing for various shows was a riveting experience. I was in my early twenties and not only learning more about myself through the country, but also how to be responsible for my dancers' safety, and to make sure they get the most out of this experience. This responsibility weighed on my shoulders. I took this seriously and knew it was a unique opportunity to not mess up.

The last trip I refer to is one of the adventures I took with my husband, Greg. Together, we have been to Italy several times over the years. For this book, I focus on a particular excursion where we toured Bologna, Florence, and Rome together. Through much research and networking, I made contact with a few dance teachers who lived in Italy with expansive knowledge about traditional Italian folk dances. I discuss learning various Tarantellas in my first book, *La Danza – Conflict, Passion and Healing.* The first Italian dance instructor I met was in the United States. At that time, my dance company was only about six years old, and I was searching desperately for more authentic dances from different regions. It's extremely challenging to find these dances in the United States since it's not written down or preserved well enough.

The goal I set back then was to collect a dance from all twenty regions. I was a member of an Italian organization that held conferences around the United States each year. This particular year, it was going to be held in a city that was just a few hours from us. Greg agreed to go with me and be my dance partner so I could learn and acquire more dances. Filled with nervous excitement, we packed our bags and ventured out on a two-hour drive and checked into the hotel for the conference. This three-day event was filled with all things about Italian culture, the folk costumes, authentic music, dance and folk-art crafts. Once registered, we could choose what classes or events we wanted to attend. Of course, we signed up for all the dance classes. I was impressed and elated Greg was willing to learn these dances with me. We weren't even married yet at the time. For me, this gesture clearly demonstrated he was in it for the long haul.

Meeting this dance instructor was the catalyst and gave me the confidence I needed to seek out other instructors in Italy that held the key to unlock dances I was hoping to preserve. Federica was her name. She was a dance instructor flown in from Milan and was the featured guest at the conference. Being from Milan, she had studied intensely at the university as well as conservatories in music and theater. She collaborated on numerous projects with Italian theater groups as well as musicians concerning theater and dance. Federica had a vast amount of knowledge about dances from various northern regions of Italy and I was astounded by her accomplishments. As I walked into the grand ballroom of the conference hotel, I recognized her immediately by the way she was standing. She had long golden silky hair and a petite stature with a confident posture. Greg noticed the twinkle in my eyes. She would be my first official dance instructor from Italy. We hurried and found a table and placed our things down on one of the chairs. My dance shoes went on like there was a fire drill. I grabbed Greg's arm to get a perfect spot on the dance floor for the class that was about to start. It felt as if she was going to reveal some sort of secret to all the dances I had struggled to find. I waited on bated breath for her to speak.

The conference director introduced her, and she was received with a warm friendly applause. After a few moments went by, she walked over to the center of the ballroom and said "*Andiamo*!" Let's go! Everyone gathered around to start warming up their bodies to begin this long day of learning. She got straight down to business and started demonstrating the first set of steps to a dance right away. Her teaching style was precise, no nonsense, yet filled with a sense of joy and pride.

Her confidence and passion were evident. Her sparkling smile didn't fool me; she meant business and was ready to make us sweat. The instant she raised her arms to show us the proper hold with our partners was like a bird gliding through the sky. Her grace and elegance were visible. Since Greg is so tall, I was holding on to his bicep instead of his shoulder. He kept up and doing his best to assist me. I promised him it would be fun, and this learning would pay off. He enjoyed just being with me, he said. Spending this weekend together really showed me he was not only going to be a great dance partner, but also a partner for life. Building trust with a partner is crucial in life and on the dance floor.

This dance workshop lasted all day with breaks every hour or so. Learning several dances from different northern regions was overwhelming, but doable with notes. From time to time, I checked in with Greg since dance can be challenging. He was a real trooper to hang in there. I know he was exhausted and wanted to find a lounge to chill out with a cold beverage. I don't blame him, these dances required great concentration and control. I was proud of him and grateful for his willingness to participate in my never-ending saga of preservation.

After a few hours of dancing, I was hyped from learning so much information. I didn't know which would burst first, my head or my heart. These kinds of opportunities are hard to find and when I come across them, I know they can set me on a path that is going to be transformative. Feeling deep in my bones this conference was going to change the direction of my research, my skin tingled with curiosity.

Federica taught about five or six elegant dances that day from various regions. I was checking them off one at a time like a bingo card. I could see this conference was getting me closer to all twenty regions. At one point during the session, I noticed she paused to watch me briefly as I practiced a few steps. She came over to compliment me and struck up a conversation. We exchanged dance credentials, and I explained my goal of preservation. She was thrilled for me and gave me some advice along with a book she wrote which contained the dance notes. She autographed the book with the phrase "Dance is Beautiful."

Greg smiled at her in hopes she would offer a compliment to him too since he was giving it his all. But instead, she kindly nodded at him and walked on. I explained to Greg not everyone gets compliments. I assured him he was doing a great job despite not hearing from the instructor. It's always an honor to receive a compliment from a teacher, but this compliment was very special to me. She was praising my Italian dance steps. Compliments are like a piece of candy, receiving them all the time isn't good, but sparingly offered is remembered and savored. We tend to learn more from our failures than our achievements. I was thrilled to be performing the steps correctly.

These bright and graceful dances she taught were from the Italian renaissance, precisely done with calculated steps and deliberate formations. We stayed in perfect lines that transformed into squares or brief circles, all timed with the music.

Northern dances were a vast departure from the southern dances I grew up with as a child. The southern tarantellas are wild, organic, and free flowing where you move into the center of a dance circle for a moment while others cheer you on and back out on a whim. There are no counts for a specific move or military-like formations. You change formations in the south when the spirit moves you or when a leader gives a whistle or call. The northern dances were a delightful addition to my collection and showed me a fresh side of Italy I couldn't wait to explore further.

5,6,7,8

- Who have you met that set you on a path?
- Do you take chances in life? If so, when?
- What actions or gestures make a good partner?
- What lessons have you learned from visiting the same place?

A small souvenir book from Milan that contained photos and facts.

Milan

At the age of twelve, I was unaware of how deep my mom's grief was until I was approaching fifty myself and now left without my parents here. You never feel like you have enough time on Earth to spend with your loved ones. There are so many questions I wanted to ask and events I wanted my family to be a part of in some way. I believe my mom longed for more time with her parents and searched for a pathway to answers. She, like me, was struggling with so many questions about her family that my ancestors had left behind. Love and grief were driving forces to gain answers that could ease her pain and bring her closure. This would be the one and only time my mother traveled to Italy. Because of her health over the years, she was unable to return.

As I recall this first trip, it was an extremely crucial moment in both her life and in mine.

My sixth-grade school year was ending, and I was leaving my child like days behind. My mom decided my older brother, Stephen, and I would join her on this adventure to meet our family in Italy as well as see more of the country. We were traveling at the same time as my grade school graduation, but I didn't mind not attending it at all. I was thrilled to go to Italy, yet nervous because of so many unknowns. It was my first plane ride and train ride and going out of the United States at this point in my life.

My brother Stephen is seven years older than I am and is a talented musician. His fingers have never met a piano which he couldn't play. He has been blessed with an artistic gift and can play almost any song by ear. Many years of piano lessons were paying off for him greatly. He too was excited to go on this adventure with our mom.

So many experiences and life altering moments would come from this journey. My mom asked me if I wanted to get my ears pierced before we travel to commemorate my graduation. I was eager to get my first pair of earrings. She also decided to get her ears pierced with me. It made a great bonding experience and prepared us for a copious amount of firsts together. We chose our birthstones to be our first pair of studs.

I packed my clothes into a small suitcase along with a pocket size notebook that my father suggested I should bring. He didn't travel with us so he could take care of our home and my sweet dog. His service in the army took him all over Europe. He encouraged me to jot down my voyage to capture memories. I am so glad I listened to his advice. Each time I travel, I take notes and photos along the way to recall the experiences and lessons learned. After a few connecting flights, we landed in Milan.

Once we arrived, I was swept away by the sights, smells, sounds and the vastness of the city. I can certainly see why it is the birthplace of espresso. This city is on the go all the time. Sounds that every big city has: the traffic, the trains, people chatting in various languages, and restaurants setting up their tables and chairs outside consumed the sound waves everywhere. This bustling city, located in the Lombardy region, has its finger on the pulse of design, fashion and finance. I couldn't wait to dive into all of it.

Milan is known for high fashion, and it was obvious. Photos of models on various covers of magazines were at every newsstand. Window shopping was something my mom and I enjoyed. It's where we would get the best ideas and inspiration for decorating our house or how to dress. When something caught our eye, we would go into the shop.

On the plane, I created a wish list of items I wanted to purchase while in Italy. Two of the items included an Italian doll and a fashionable silk scarf. Not long after we ventured out in the city, I spotted a small doll that was dressed in a traditional dance costume from that region. My mom also found a beautiful silk scarf for me to add to my purchase. Walking out of the shop, I immediately tossed it on. Wearing the scarf around my neck or tied around my purse strap made me feel like a local model.

A girl can dream!

As we continued around the main piazza, I began taking in the colors of everything from the buildings to fashion and even the table settings. Paying attention to details is one of my superpowers that I was starting to develop. I made a note of the details in my notebook. My listening skills were also improving each day from listening to people speaking Italian and trying to translate in my head. Hearing the church bells chime their delightful tunes added a lovely sound in my ears. Music can spark great memories.

We had a couple of long days of sight-seeing and shopping. We packed so much in a short amount of time, but it was all worth the effort. With all this touring, I was convinced my feet were going to fall off. The three of us chatted about the itinerary for the next day. It was filled with more sights and miles of walking so sleep was necessary. We arrived back at our wonderful hotel where our room was situated a few floors up. It was a cozy space to relax and take in the city from above.

After I washed the day off in the shower, I jumped into comfortable pajamas and crawled into bed. No sheep counting for this girl, I fell fast asleep. In my restful slumber, I was awakened by startling noises. I sat up to listen closely to try to figure out what it was. It was after midnight and sounded like chanting or maybe singing. I was unsure. I nudged my mother as any child would do. She awoke in a slight panic. She thought I was sick or had a nightmare. But then she heard it too.

Looking at me she whispered, "what in the world is that?"

I shrugged my shoulders. It was getting louder and louder and seemed even closer to us. Even though our room was on an upper-level floor, it felt like it was starting to vibrate with the increasing sound. I swear the walls and floor were pulsating to a beat.

We both threw the covers back and jumped to our feet. We dashed to the window and pulled back the curtains. As we looked down, we could see a massive crowd coming down the street chanting and cheering with confidence. They seemed in a great mood and were dancing a bit as they moved collectively down the street. Their arms were stuffed with bottles of wine, flags, and soccer balls.

We then realized it was the crowd from a soccer match. Their team won and the fans were celebrating by singing, dancing and chanting all the way through the city like a parade of triumph. I stared outside the window and watched them move down the street for at least ten more minutes. They looked so happy and filled with excitement.

Soccer, or *futbol* as they call it, is quite important to Italians like dance is to me. I understood their joy. To finally achieve your goal is definitely worth celebrating. Seeing more and more locals join in on their victory parade of joy was inspiring to watch. I kept thinking how wonderful it would be to be celebrated when you achieved something momentous in life.

Perhaps a parade where the whole town could join in to celebrate. That would feel so wonderful. Instead, many times we keep our 'wins' to ourselves because we don't want to boast or make people feel less than. I tend to keep many wins to myself these days. I never want to make people feel slighted. But on the other hand, celebrating achievements, no matter how small, is important. Even a small note of jubilation is a nice way to acknowledge a stepping stone.

Witnessing the community support for the team was great. These parade goers weren't on the team and didn't do any of the work to achieve that win, but they were supporting, celebrating, and feeling like a part of the community. This was the lesson I was absorbing. Despite being young at the time, I was learning that the community should celebrate wins and share it!

My mom slowly pulled me away from the window to get back to sleep. I couldn't wait for another day of unexpected events, sights and of course scrumptious food. I did my best to quiet my brain and drift off to sleep.

Besides soccer, the city of Milan is the home of high fashion. So many famous designers and artists are known for their work in this city. As a twelve-year-old girl, I was filled with the anticipation of seeing high fashion up close.

What girl doesn't want a piece of couture?

I must have consumed thousands of magazines over the years. From clothing to make up and all things that made up design, I would search for a magazine at every grocery store to buy. As a performer, costumes, sequins and rhinestones were the norm in my life. While in Milan, I was delighted to not only view the gowns in the windows, but also the fashion people were wearing on the street. Fashion can take you to a land where you have never been before or allow you to express your personality. It helps you tell the story of you. An expression of who you are and your tastes. I've heard that you should dress the part you want to be in life.

Every fairy tale I read as a child contained a princess dressed in a beautiful ball gown with gems that glistened like fresh fallen snow as she entered the room. My goal was to sparkle and shine when I made an entrance. I had an aunt that said make sure you look good both coming and going! To feel confident, glamorous, and understand you are important could be achieved with fashion. I wanted to step into that fairytale and become a *principessa*! A real princess dancing at a royal ball.

After a night of dreaming, we got an early start for more sightseeing. We arrived at the Galleria near the Cathedral, which is the world's oldest shopping mall. My eyes had a feast day on all the famous brands like Gucci, Prada and so many others showcased in every store window. My mouth dropped open as I squeezed my mom's hand. She reminded me to slow down and take in the moment, but I was zeroing in on the store windows.

It was so hard not to get caught up with the dazzling displays. The gowns were so lavish and regal, I thought for sure this is the place where all the fairy tale royalties bought their gowns. Gazing at those windows filled me with joy and inspired me to keep working towards my goals. This was just the boost I needed to keep my inspiration going. As I stood there, I knew I didn't have the funds to buy any of those gowns. My goal was to create something that others would also stop and admire. It wasn't the goal to own the dress, but to be the one to create something so grand. We visited a few shops where I picked up several small souvenirs. All this retail therapy worked up an appetite. It was time for lunch!

So what about the food in Milan? From the Risotto alla Milanese to the warm hearty Minestrone, Milan has dishes everyone will savor. Besides their main courses, I looked forward to tasting some pastries and desserts. I found a delectable treat that reminded me of the holidays. Every Christmas, we buy a *panettone* or Christmas cake for dessert after our feast of the seven fishes dinner on Christmas Eve. This is just one of the many tasty treats you can find.

The *panettone* is a bread cake with lots of texture, filled with raisins and candied oranges or other fruit. Some cakes are small enough for two people or large and tall enough to feed a family. The first connection of *panettone* with Christmas was found in the Italian writings of the 18th century illuminist Pietro Verri. So much history in every bite! To this day, I seek out *panettone* to taste to remember the days my grandparents and extended family would gather around a table to celebrate the holidays together. It's just a small way you can hold onto traditions and honor those memories.

Food awakens our taste buds and evokes a nostalgia of laughter, music, dance and being together as a family. By using several of the senses, I picture being in my grandmother's kitchen, helping to roll out dough to make fresh pasta or pastries with my fingers. Meals bring us together in so many ways. The table is a place where you become a family and share your life and all that it has to offer. There is so much love rolled into a meal at the table. When we sit down to eat, everyone is equal. Milan is no different than any other city in Italy where food is emotional, memorable, and embedded in their daily lives.

From the taste buds to the ear buds, Milan has a particularly famous musical tradition, being the home of several important composers such as Giuseppe Verdi. Born in 1813, Verdi was known for his operas such as *Rigoletto* or *Aida*. His operas have become an essential operatic repertoire around the world. I never attended an opera as a child, but I watched a few on television over the years. Going to the opera is something that many elites would attend. Operas tell beautiful and dramatic stories like ballets and share the works of some of the greatest musicians and composers.

In 1778, an opera house called La Scala was built to showcase some of the most outstanding operas and ballets. You will find this gorgeous opera house theater built on the site of the church of Santa Maria della Scala. *Scala* in Italian means staircase. I felt as if I was taking another step towards my career as a dancer by seeing this incredible theater. Visiting La Scala was on my vision board, and I couldn't wait to check this one off my list.

My mother, brother and I were standing outside admiring the beautiful building. So many famous opera singers have graced the stage over the years. The hairs on my arms stood at attention when walking inside. My brother and I slowly wandered closer to the stage to get a better look at it. My brother, the musician, and I, the dancer, were itching to perform. There was a janitor standing on the side of the stage sweeping and tidying the theater. He could see where we were salivating to further the fantasy. My mother gestured politely and asked if we could go onto the stage to look around. He outstretched his arm to welcome us up to the stage to enjoy. I dashed to the center of the stage and stopped abruptly to face the audience.

My eyes became wide as I looked up towards the balcony. There, at the top, I was met by the sculpted ceilings, red velvet seats and a grand chandelier. Imagining the theater packed with an audience, I began my performance. It's the moment any dancer desires, to perform on a grand stage such as this one. My arms floated upward with a slow *port de bra* while one of my legs began a *developé* which led into a few pirouettes. I continued into a solo ballet improv as if I was a prima ballerina. My brother found a piano nearby to tickle the ivories and accompany my performance.

We just couldn't help ourselves. For just a glorious moment, we were performing on a stage that was historical and profound. As any proud parent would do, our mom burst into applause and cheered us on. She, too, was caught up in the fantasy. The janitor chimed in with an uplifting whistle to show his joy. My brother hit his final chord and I struck a final pose. The janitor shouted "Bravissimo!" Perhaps our performance brought a little joy to his day of work. I know it brightened our day for sure.

Imagination keeps our dreams alive. *Doesn't it?* A few minutes on that stage was all the time needed to motivate me with dance. It filled my soul to stand where all the famous ballets were performed. Every artist's dream is to stand in the spotlight where so many historical performances took place.

My brother raised his fingers from the keys as I took a noble curtsy to collect my imaginary roses being thrown at me. Thoughts raced that day dreaming of what it would be like to be a part of the ballet academy at La Scala. What an incredible moment and place to explore. I was picturing Carla Fracci, an Italian ballet dancer from Milan, performing on that stage. She was considered one of the greatest ballerinas of the 20th century. I admired many of her photographs in my dance books. She died in 2021 but left quite a legacy behind. A leading dancer of La Scala Theatre Ballet in Milan, she worked with various other international companies including the Royal Ballet, Royal Swedish Ballet and American Ballet Theatre. Her interpretation of leading roles was commended in several romantic ballets, such as La Sylphide, Giselle, Swan Lake, and Romeo and Juliet. I could almost feel her presence on stage with me.

When you are young, you dream vividly, and your imagination feels so real and powerful. Do you remember sitting in your room and letting your imagination take over? Playing pretend with toys and creating an ultimate utopia where everything is achievable was my daily adventure. Thinking about all the possibilities of who I could become or where I might travel helped me discern what I liked and disliked. Using my imagination aided me to make sense of the world around me. The sky's the limit when you are young. No mountain is too high to climb or ocean too vast to sail across. The desires and ambition we hold in our mind initiates cognitive growth. Exploring our passions leads us on a path to our career and a better life.

I would consistently picture dancing on stage and an audience applauding for me. When do we lose that imagination? Do we stop dreaming or wishing at a specific age?

Why do people discourage the young to stop dreaming or to not think they can achieve anything? I am so thankful my parents encouraged me to never stop thinking the sky's the limit. Don't get me wrong, they explained realistically I needed a job to make a living so I could survive.

I have always held down several jobs and gigs to make ends meet. My parents stood beside me while I pursued my passion for dance and picked me up when I failed at achieving a goal. Rather than discourage me, they gave me the tools I needed to survive and thrive. Showing me that there is always another path to try when I fail. Learning from our failures is far more important than celebrating our wins. Seeking an alternate route to succeed gives me hope. Hope is the quality that keeps my dreams alive.

Believing in yourself can be challenging at times, but it's something one has to practice. To look in a dance studio mirror each day and believe you can master a difficult dance phrase or to jump higher takes courage and mental strength. Dance is both physically and mentally difficult. To keep returning and trying the same move over and over until it becomes second nature requires determination and the will to be better.

We are never too old to dream a bigger dream. In fact, most of the time, as artists, we are told to give it up and not to waste our time on it. Throughout my career, I often heard that same phrase. I was even told that being a dancer isn't a "*real*" job. Yes, it is a real job! My feet know it's real, trust me. It's a tremendous amount of work, hard work, with a great purpose.

I believe that anything can be achieved one step at a time. With dance, we are required to do one step at a time; it is how we progress. Learning step by step reveals to me my growth and promise in small segments. This gives me hope when I need it. Small achievements show me improvements and that my goals are within reaching distance. That boost of confidence gives me the energy to keep going and achieve more in dance, in my research and in life.

While my mother's applause for my impromptu performance on stage lingered in my mind, I was still floating on air as we left the theater.

I felt that the city of Milan held that same grit and determination, where the opportunities were endless. The music, dance, theater and fashion were all a part of an art explosion and perhaps I found my art utopia in real life. It was comforting to be surrounded by this type of creativity and see the hard work pay off.

Being so inspired at that young age spurred on a flurry of projects and countless inspirational moments for me. Once I discovered these hidden gems in Italy, I couldn't ignore them. I began to look for them everywhere like an Easter egg in a video game or movie. If you open up yourself to being creative, you will start to see life in a fresh new way.

Circolo Circasso

Milan is the capital city of the region of Lombardy. Many dances such as waltzes and polkas can be found in this region. *Circolo Circasso* is a community dance that dates back to the end of the 19th century. It can also be found in England, Scotland and later spread into France as well. I learned this dance from Chiara, my dance instructor in Naples, Italy. She knew my quest to find dances from all twenty regions of Italy. So she chose this northern dance to share with me since it was fairly easy to perform and teach to others.

The dance begins in a circle filled with couples holding hands. Everyone takes four steps forward towards the center of the circle and four steps back. The ladies break from holding hands and take four steps in with a slight curtsy and then four steps back to return. The men then take four steps in and stretch their arms to give high fives to the other men in the center at the same time. As the men take their four steps back out, they turn to face their lady and interlock both hands and begin rotating as a couple with a step ball-change step, or gallop. Then the couple assumes a promenade posture where all couples promenade in a big circle using a chasing step to travel. After about sixteen counts, the lady unwinds from her partner and the circle is reset to start the sequence of steps again.

Each round has a unique hold or partner connection when the man finishes his four steps in and four steps out to connect with his lady. Usually, a handshake with one hand while the other hand connects at the hip of the lady. Other times it's a handshake with one hand while the other hand is on the partner's opposite shoulder. *Circolo* has a community spirit with a flair of ease to the movements. The 4/4 tempo makes it easy to count and join in. It was simple to memorize the sequence of steps which made it comforting and welcoming to participate. It is gratifying to teach this dance to all ages of students because of the simplistic steps and patterns of the dance form.

When my dance company performs this dance, we usually get about four rounds in and then all dancers take a walk in a circle sixteen steps right and left. Then we break to snake the circle to a line so that each dancer can take a bow individually.

We have performed this dance consistently now in various parts of the United States and it always brings joy to the crowd. When we offer this dance as part of our choreography seminars, the students or community members catch on easily and really seem to enjoy the pedestrian aspect of it. I can see their confidence grow as we get to the second or third round and their posture becomes taller. They start walking lighter and carry their shoulders back like they are part of the royal court. To me, this is where the magic begins, that moment it clicks, and everyone starts to feel in sync. The power is felt in this moment when a group can work as one and not break stride or veer off course.

We all desire to feel confident the moment we make decisions in life. Confidence flourishes when we have a team or group with us that supports us by holding our hands through the most difficult times in our lives. People who are ready to celebrate our achievements and be a part of our success are the people we want in our circle. These are the lessons this particular dance has taught me. *Circolo* is a dance of everyday life where you must carry your head held high like you have a crown on and work hand in hand with others to make a difference.

We now must leave the dance floor and catch a train to Venice. In the next chapter you will see the city through not only my young eyes, but also unmask this floating fantasy in my twenties when I toured with my dance company.

5,6,7,8

- Have you experienced something strange on a trip?
- How do you celebrate your wins?
- What memories do you have with food?
- Do you daydream? If so, about what?

My necklace that was bought on Murano Island.

Venice

Our next stop was Venice, a city without roads, in the Veneto region. About a three-hour train ride from Milan, heading east, the mood changes from a hustle and bustle tempo to a tranquil ambiance. I loved traveling on the train seeing the small towns passing by outside my window.

Some people call Venice the city of canals, to which I agree. Traveling around Venice requires a willingness to walk or ride a boat of some sort. With 118 small islands and over four hundred bridges, this floating paradise leaves you with an art gallery level of photos with every click.

With so much to take in, where do I start?

I have visited Venice a few times since I was twelve, but that first journey to Venice with my mom and brother was memorable. Once we were off the train, we settled into our hotel. My brother and I were excited to explore the city. My mother wasn't thrilled about traveling by boat, however. We wandered around the famous piazza *San Marco* or St. Mark's Square. This main heartbeat of Venice dates back to the ninth century. We visited *San Marco Basilica, Campanile di San Marco* and *Doge's Palace*, to get a sense of the area. It's all in the same square along with a large flock of pigeons to greet us.

Dancing with a few pigeons as we crossed the *piazza*, we paced ourselves to digest this city in just a few days. Seeing these outstanding places can be intense and mentally exhausting from all the history that hits you like a ton of bricks. I remember hearing so many facts and figures at every place or museum, my mind would go numb. It's hard to remember everything, but my trusty journal kept the highlights daily. I felt like a reporter or investigator on the job. I couldn't wait to share everything I learned with my dad when I returned.

Campanile di San Marco is a staggering three-hundred-and twenty-three-foot tall bell tower and is the most recognizable structure of the Venetian skyline. It was used as a watch tower in the past and even though lions don't roam throughout the city anymore, you will find a statue of one at the top. I took a beat or two to stretch my legs as I looked up at the mountain of stairs I was about to climb. My brother and I began the climb to the top. My mother had a look of terror on her face. Having a fear of heights and drowning, this city was her least favorite. She never expressed her fears to us in words, but I could tell by the look on her face and her grip on my hand, she was terrified. My brave mom hung in there with us to not disappoint. Deep breaths were used on the climb upward where a spectacular view of the city awaited us! I could hear my mother breathing forcefully as we got closer to the top.

Inhale and exhale.

Gaining more muscles as I climbed the hundreds of steps to get to the top of the bell tower, my legs were telling me this was a mistake. However, my curiosity wanted to make it to the top to see what Galileo once saw. Galileo di Vincenzo Bonaiuti de' Galilei was born in 1564, he was an Italian astronomer, physicist and engineer from Pisa. He used this campanile as an observatory to study the skies and it was there in1609 that he demonstrated his telescope to the royals.

Come on, who doesn't want to walk in the footsteps of Galileo? Talk about star quality!

Once we arrived at the top, the skyline was everything. Taking in the extraordinary views of all of Venice, one discovers how small in life you truly are seeing from a different perspective. Being so short, I realized how small I was comparing myself to the statues at the top. Walking to one side, I began scanning the entire city slowly. I was taking a mental picture of the landscape. Being close to the edge of the tower made my mother nervous. However, she had to admit how impressive the stunning picturesque site was and proud she faced her fear of heights. We were all learning lessons on this expedition. Now, all we had to do was walk back down. Let's just say, we earned a gelato that afternoon.

Once we got back to our hotel, looking up at the sky that night, my mind kept thinking more about Galileo, the stars and astronomy. I wrote in my journal, "the sky actually is the limit."

The next day, we set out for San Marco Basilica, the Catholic church and Archdiocese of Venice. No photos are allowed to be taken inside, but it is free to tour and worth the visit. Once you walk in, you will be greeted by gold tiles from the ceiling to the flooring. Everything had a holy golden hue to it. The church is gorgeous and filled with outstanding paintings and mosaics. You will also catch a glimpse of St. Marks tomb for which the square is named.

Once we were finished touring the bottom of the church, we ventured to travel upstairs to the terraces. Our interests peaked to see views from above. Here we go with the steps again.

You can make it legs!

What a workout! With each step, I was filled with even more wonder. From seeing sites at the top of the bell tower, I could only imagine what I will see this time. Sure enough, we arrived at the top where a breath-taking panorama was revealed like a 3-D painting to me. I realized at this point, I was catching some of my mother's fear of heights, but I was distracted by the mesmerizing view. Seeking out the various bell towers and buildings, along with the gondolas slowly drifting far in the distance, helped calm my nerves.

From my point of view, it was like someone took a paint brush and created a grand view of what a kingdom would look like. For a small amount of time, I had a pigeon's point of view. How lucky are the pigeons to get to see this every day? It was clear how the city was laid out from that vantage point. This could be where my exuberance for maps began.

Noticing the details of the tops of the buildings got my attention. The architecture and design details were well thought out; it seemed as if the city was putting on a fashion show with the buildings as their models. It was starting to all click together for me. Seeing patterns in detail from food to fashion to architecture was starting to make sense. Noticing these patterns will later on become a feature in my choreography. This is where I became aware that design made a difference. Artistic designs and touches were everywhere in everything! It became a game to find a design in a building or bridge.

As we wandered the streets of Venice, we came across the famous *Rialto Bridge*. This bridge is iconic to the city where everyone stops at the halfway point to get that perfect photo. We watched countless people capture that moment. I believe it is impossible to take a bad photo in Italy, especially in Venice. Every photo I have captured on my vacations have always turned out like a painting. Pausing on the bridge, we were able to take in the view from both sides. Gazing at the boats traveling in and out, as well as seeing the water glistening and reflecting the bright colors of the buildings, made my mind reflect on my young life a bit. I counted the forty-two steps on each side of the bridge that came to a peak in the middle. They are wide enough for a few people to pass so it's easy to walk across.

My advice while in Venice: stop on this bridge, breathe, capture the moment with a photo and dream a little. I paused to make a wish on the bridge to return to Italy. I didn't want to take any chances of never returning. I can now say that my wish came true.

We were experiencing Venice in the spring, we never toured during the winter months. However, there is an event that could change my mind for my next excursion. It's called Carnevale, the most internationally known and oldest festival. The congregation of masked citizens always gather before the Lenten season with a grand celebration of food, fireworks, and lavish costumes like a grand ball. This is not how my family kicked off the start of the forty days of Lent before Easter. Perhaps we should give it a try. What a delight it would be to design a Met Gala-like outfit with a Renaissance flair and parade about the city to celebrate. This is going on my vision board undoubtedly!

This traditional celebration began in the 15th century and continues still today. An extravaganza event lasting ten days in which people dress up, proceed in organized parades, or simple promenades about the city. The costumes are Venetian outfits and look like they stepped out of a painting by Canaletto. Today you can rent costumes and participate in the celebrations!

You can't escape riding a boat of some sort in this city. It was time to travel to one of the islands nearby. One of the places a gondolier suggested was the island of Murano. The three of us traveled by water taxi to the island. It took about twenty minutes to reach the island. My mother, facing her fear of water, was beyond terrified about this ride, but again, she put on her brave face and let her excitement overcome her fear. Ah, with the wind in my face and the breeze blowing my hair and scarf to the side, I felt like a movie star. I was channeling my best Sophia Loren that day.

Murano Island was a prosperous commercial port from the 7th to 13th centuries. Today, it is known for glassmaking, which, like the gondoliers, is an art that has been passed down through the same families for generations.

I was warned by my mother to not touch anything since it was all made of glass. She only had to give my brother and I that look once. If you grew up in an Italian household, then you know that with one look, your behavior must be top notch. Her eyes said everything we needed to know.

We wandered about the area peeking into all the unique shops and art displays. The factories that made this blown glass were moved from Venice to Murano Island to prevent fires since many of the buildings were made of wood on the mainland. This was a brilliant idea if you ask me.

We visited quite a few establishments and observed one of the workers blow glass that day. What a spectacular showcase of wonder! Their movements are tedious and timed perfectly like a ballet with a symphony. One wrong move and the entire work of art is a shattered hot mess. I was fascinated and impressed.

Each boutique had everything from chandeliers, mirrors, drinking glasses, art decor and of course, stunning jewelry. Each artistic threshold we crossed, my mother's stern looks continued to remind me to not touch anything, but she could tell that the temptation to explore everything with my fingers was building. I barely could resist some of the décor. It looked like tasty candy because of the perfect glossy shine and swirls of colors. There were lollipops and hard candy pieces. If I didn't know it was glass, I think I would have taken a bite or two.

My eyes soaked up the array of hues of each product like a sponge. Everywhere we went, we were greeted with splashes of color. As if I walked into a rainbow, many of the designs had colors that were mixed or marbleized in some capacity. Beholding the bright colors seamlessly swirled together would brighten anyone's darkest day. Spending countless hours gazing at these pieces of art would have been fine with me. Such stunning figures and shapes, I was completely baffled how they were made from glass. Inspired by the process, innovation, and of course the creativity, my mind began to envision the dances I could create from seeing the glass blown.

If Cinderella was a Venetian needing glass slippers, what would her slippers look like if they were made on this island? Certainly, they would be more intriguing than the unimaginative transparent shoes portrayed in the story. I envisioned a perfectly sculpted pair with swirling shades of soft blue, like the water in the Venetian canals with a hue of gold, mixed with reds, like the sunsets.

What a girl wouldn't give to have a pair of glass slippers to dance the night away…if only they wouldn't break, especially as demanding as I am on shoes. I was overjoyed that my mother took us on this adventure. This island seemed to be sprinkled with pure magic.

Before the sun dipped into the water, a necklace caught my eye. Wrapped with the island's bright colors, these necklaces were made of beads that were hand painted and strung together to create a lovely ring of joy around anyone's neck. I felt compelled to touch it. I must. My mother carefully chose one for me to buy. After our purchase, I immediately placed it around my neck.

Each bead was hand painted with flowers and star bursts on it. The predominant colors were orange, blue and green with a few hints of yellow and red. It was made of thirty-seven beads and has become one of my prized pieces. I enjoy wearing it with a solid-colored shirt, so its brightness becomes the star of the outfit. Cinderella got it wrong with the shoes, and besides, she lost one. This necklace is a hundred times better, and I know what would happen to me if I lost it. Feeling like I was a Venetian princess at Carnevale, I beamed from ear to ear for the entire boat ride back to Venice.

The three of us continued on to spend time in Florence and Rome. From Rome we took another plane ride to Calabria, the toe of the boot. We were greeted there by our cousins anxiously awaiting our arrival to begin a beautiful conversation about family. This part of the quest was filled with an array of emotions from sorrow to joy. We had years to catch up on. My cousins even took me to school for a day to be fully immersed in language, culture and education.

We laughed, played games, ate delectable food and more importantly, connected as a family. This is the one and only time I met Great-Uncle Rosario. His demeanor and personality resemble my grandfather. Both he and my mother's eyes watered the moment they met. From that day on, letters, calls, and most recently video chats are as often as possible. We never want to miss a moment of each other's lives again. These were the family members that were left behind when my grandparents came to the United States. Since they never saw their family again, every time I connect with them, I feel my grandparents get a chance to live on through me.

Traditions are important and can carry a great amount of weight. I was immensely grateful my mother bought me a piece of fashion or jewelry for this important milestone. This was becoming one of our special traditions my mother was creating. Growing up, she gifted me a piece of jewelry of some sort to commemorate a special moment or occasion in my life. This adventure was surely a special occasion. Instead of my sixth-grade graduation, I was traveling through Italy! This tradition of jewelry became pieces that captured memories over time. She knew how special these artifacts in my life would become. Over the years, various dance pins, bracelets and necklaces have represented dance recitals, graduations, festival performances and so many other noteworthy moments. A fine collection in my jewelry box now encapsulates numerous memories and achievements. Beauty was found in many forms in Venice, from seeing the stars as Galileo did, watching blown glass take shape, or picking out jewelry that connects with family. Beauty surrounded my journey.

Dressed in my costume for a photo in Venice.

Years later, in my twenties, I was touring with my dance company to Venice, Florence, Montecatini and Rome. Since we were in Venice, I was thinking about Carnevale. While costume ideas were swirling in my mind, one of my dancers nudged me about a small shop that made masks. Stepping inside the shop, I was met with an artist who was amid painting a mask. I was taken back with the vast variety of mask creations that were hanging on the wall in the shop. Masks of all sorts and sizes, some with long noses or small dainty ones with lace that covered the eyes. The ones layered with fabric and ribbons and bits of dangling jewelry were unprecedented. Instantly, at least five of them became my favorites. I was perplexed about which to choose. While I wanted to take them all home, I could never afford that many nor had room to spare in my suitcase.

Faced with a final decision, I started to narrow down my favorites. While gathering my choices in hand, out of the corner of my eye, I became intrigued with the man painting a fresh mask. He had such concentration and a look of intensity on his face. The finest detail went into each and every stroke he made with a brush fit for Barbie to use. I didn't want to disturb him, but I had so many burning questions I wanted to ask. My curiosity pushed me to start a conversation.

I slowly walked up to him and softly introduced myself so as to not to jolt his hand. Looking up over his glasses, he kindly broke away from his painting to attend to me. As we were conversing, he mentioned that he just made some masks for a movie in America. What an incredible opportunity meeting this talented artist! We bonded over creative interests since we are both artists in different ways.

He explained mask making happened around the 12th century. The process of resin is by adding wet papers covered with glue in layers like a lasagna. Masks and Carnevale celebrations were banned throughout history by Napoleon and Mussolini. In the 1970s, a small group of artisans picked up the craft again to bring it back. The attention to detail along with the repetition gives the technique new life. After the masks are dry, the details are added like paint, jewelry, or even 24k gold leaf.

His talent was evident, and I was pleased to hear that his work was being seen and celebrated in a movie. I congratulated him on his beautiful work and made a mask purchase. I told him the masks were for my dancers to wear for a future performance. I was already sketching out the choreography. It was gratifying to purchase a work of art I saw being created in front of me. I thanked him for showing me his creative process. I was inspired by the mask-making history lesson.

His creations stood out beautifully on stage. A little piece of his life at that snapshot in time is now a piece of my history. What a sweet sentiment to know his work allowed my work to bloom. As I look at my masks today, the memory of meeting the artist that made them lights up my soul.

His attention to every detail and repetitive motion resonated with me as a dancer. Our minds must be concentrating on our movement with each nuance from how to hold our arms and fingers down to pointing or flexing our feet. The repetitive motion of movements allows our bodies to memorize the choreography to become second nature on stage. This is the reason when you see an artist in their element, they make it look so easy. It is because they have a great deal of experience. The word *sprezzatura*, means a graceful performance without any effort. This is the best way I can describe what I witnessed. Artists make it look so effortless and easy to accomplish. When there are years of laboring, learning, and concentration that is done.

I guess we all wear a mask from time to time in our lives. Don't we? At work or school, we put on an imaginary facade when we are not feeling ourselves. What about when we first meet someone? We put on a facade to impress them. As a dancer, yes, we transform into a character or creature of some sort on stage that isn't who we really are. We are pretending or acting as well as dancing. Although, I tend to find some truth in all movements. When we move, we are revealing a layer of realness as that particular character or emotion we are portraying. Our bodies travel throughout the space to seek truth and relay this message back to the audience.

During the pandemic, I stared at the masks that I bought in Venice comparing it to the masks I was now having to wear. Buying cloth or N-95 masks to protect myself from a virus. I guess history is repeated often. During the Black Plague, the Venetians created these masks to hide the ugliness that the bubonic plague did to their faces. But more importantly, they used the masks to diffuse the smell of the plague.

The Black Death, which hit Europe in 1347, claimed over 25 million lives in just four years. The plague arrived in Europe when twelve ships from the Black Sea docked at the Sicilian port of Messina. The cause was a bacteria that was from fleas from animals and rodents.

Reflecting upon the countless lives lost around the world due to the CoronaVirus, I felt as if I was living in historical times again. Going out and wearing a mask has now become a part of my wardrobe. The urge to dress up in a Carnevale outfit and Venetian mask to stroll into the grocery store or just to pick up the mail is real. But I will save this idea for the next parade we dance in or a Halloween party.

Some of the black plague masks had a long-beak shape, which would give the air sufficient time to be diffused by the protective herbs before it hit plague doctors' nostrils and lungs. Envision placing herbs and dried flowers to create a pleasant scent in the mask. What herbs or flowers would you put inside your mask? I would have chosen the herb rosemary and perhaps lily of the valley. Those are my favorite.

Traveling in Venice by water taxi, gondola or ferry brought many emotions to mind. Feeling the tranquility with an undertone of a quiet hustle going on, the clear blue water crashing against the edge near the colorful houses and buildings gave me beach vibes. It's a relaxing city to sight see, listen and people watch while dining at an outdoor cafe. With countless bridges and streets to get lost in, one can find copious amounts of shops and sites with a rich history to absorb.

Dressed in their horizontally striped shirts and straw-like hats with a red ribbon flowing from the side, the gondoliers go about their day with pride and determination. Like a morning bird, their songs are heard daily as they paddle their way under each arching bridge. Gondoliers take pride in their job. With well-rehearsed choreography, I watched them arrive at the dock and prepare for the day ahead. Some are lifting heavy crates and boxes onto the boats while others are delivering goods to different parts of the city. Then a long line of gondoliers wait to offer rides for tourists.

Taking a ride can be romantic, especially if you are with someone you love. I can see why so many people take time to do this ride. It's on everyone's list when they visit Venice. The calm serenity feeling washes over the mind and body as you view the surroundings from a different perspective. It is pure heaven to just float.

When touring Venice with my dance company, I wanted to see their faces as they experienced a gondola ride for the first time. I know it's a bit touristy, but there is an entertaining element to the ride as the gondoliers share their favorite spots to eat or visit. They make great impromptu tour guides and are good sports about taking photos and making lifetime memories for the travelers. Our gondolier graciously offered his hand to help us in and out of the boat since it was a little scary and unstable when you take your first step. Just like in life, it's nice to have someone lend you a hand when things are unstable.

One at a time, the dancers carefully stepped into the gondola and slowly sat down on the velvet padded seat. A few of the dancers got into one gondola with me and the rest of them stepped into the second one.

Swoosh!

The gondolier pushed off with his large paddle and our excursion began.

As we made our way through the canals, our gondolier sang a heavenly song in Italian. All of us were clapping and singing along with him as our voices echoed underneath the bridges. Maybe we weren't the best singers, but the choral moment filled our hearts. After his serenade to us, he shared his personal favorite places that we should check out as a group. These bonding experiences were uniting us.

While listening to his beautiful operatic voice, it reminded me of when opera was new! In the latter part of the 16th century, a new musical style evolved leading to a drastic change that influenced the centuries that followed. Some of the greatest Renaissance composers like Claudio Monteverdi, a musician and Catholic priest, shared his talents and new concepts. His creation of echo sonatas, which are the instrumental parts with melodic lines, not the same as the choral lines, made a big impact. His innovation of this new style is what we now know as opera. This massive achievement was a new way of connecting music and words. This led to new instrumental techniques and a new conception of sound. This innovation is still studied today.

This theme is also found in the dances from this time period as well. Both ballets and operas were so dramatic and emotional. Ballet uses various sets of gestures that mean certain words similar to sign language. Instead of singing the words to tell a story like in an opera, ballet uses gestures, grand costumes and scenic designs to share a story with the audience.

Gondoliers have their own gestures and signs as they pass fellow gondoliers. Having a long family lineage in this kind of work is normal. Clearly, transportation flows through their blood and history to do this for a living like dance or the arts is in mine. Traditions of all kinds are seriously regarded by Italians. Many families have a job that is passed down from generation to generation. This consistency speaks to their pride and preservation of their history.

Craftsmen in Italy are third or fourth generations of the same family, even today. From the storefronts to fishermen, the gondoliers to cobblers, families stick together, and traditions dictate which professions young men and women will follow. First learning the trade by observing, participating, and eventually teaching their offspring, mimics the same way that traditional dances are taught. Dances are preserved by showing the next generation how to do each step carefully. I learned so many folk-dance steps as a child and today I can recall those steps easily while mastering new ones. It's tradition!

I was walking the same streets with my dancers as I did when I was twelve. It became a memory lane as I came across a brooch that my mother would adore. She fancied wearing them for her women's club meetings. At one of the shops, I discovered that brooches were originally intended to hold pieces of cloth to the body. The oldest brooches discovered date back to the Bronze Age and were made with thorns and hard quartz.

Since my mother's passing years later, along with several of my aunts, my jewelry box has expanded to include antique brooches, earrings and costume jewelry that became a collection of family mementos. While my Murano necklace is not made of diamonds or precious metals, it still makes me feel like a member of nobility.

After my dancers and I returned from our excursion that day, I requested a dance technique class for all of us. The tour guide found a local dance studio and hired an accomplished instructor to fulfill my request. The dancers changed clothes and waited in the lobby of our hotel to be picked up by our tour guide. Arriving at the studio filled with a jumble of nerves, we walked up a set of stairs to a lavishly designed dance studio.

Our instructor warmly greeted and invited us in to get settled. It was immediately evident to me that she was a classically, well-trained ballerina that most likely performed at

La Scala in Milan. She surprised us by offering a modern jazz class to change it up and be creative. Possibly, she was ready to let go of her ballet bun and explore something different. We enjoyed the class and learned a great deal of style from her. It wasn't what we expected at all. Staring at her tall, beautiful physique she shared a resume as extensive as a library. I was right, she did perform at La Scala! She was precise and creative. I was thankful for the technique class, corrections and feedback as well as the chance to give my muscles a proper stretch before venturing onto our next city to perform.

We thanked her for the class and asked to take a quick photo with her before leaving. She was kind enough to share her smile with us so we could save the moment. We turned to curtsy and bow to her for being our teacher. At the end of any dance class, it is proper to thank the teacher and curtsy or bow to show respect. This act of acknowledgment stems straight from the history of ballet. I always encourage students to thank the teacher at the end of any learning session. My dancers understand I take gratitude practice very seriously. This is part of their training and perhaps a great life lesson to enforce. Remembering that teachers come and go in your life in many forms from parents, instructors or shopkeepers. One can always learn something valuable from various sources.

Our days in Venice vanished so fast, like melting *gelato*. Our visit was filled with museums that contained a copious number of Egyptian artifacts and an exploration of churches that lifted our souls. We made wishes on almost every bridge we walked across and admired buskers on the streets sharing their sunny melodies or painting their masterpieces. I wanted my dancers to absorb the history and witness the culture in action, so that the next time we performed, they felt connected to the traditions from the moment their feet hit the stage. Even though not all the dancers on this tour were of Italian descent, I saw their eyes sparkle and a fire of appreciation in their hearts.

Perfetto!

The dancers and I continued on to explore Florence, Montecatini and finally Rome where we performed for the Pope! This exciting opportunity to perform as well as study is a time not taken for granted. It was thrilling and unforgettable. I speak more about that day in my first book.

A city unparalleled, where bridges connect the past with the present day, Venice is, by far, one of the most extraordinary cities I have visited. With a bit of mystery, elegance and a serene environment, this floating city reels me in consistently. I look forward to roaming the streets again and discovering more remarkable history.

La Furlana

Found in the Veneto region of Italy, I came across this dance from a dance expert named Elba. When I was in college, I did a lengthy interview over the phone with her about authentic Italian dances for my college thesis. The internet wasn't around yet and calling was the quickest way I could get the information. It was also very costly at the time since calling long distance cost a fortune. But, I saved up my phone points and used them up on just this one lengthy phone call.

Elba had studied in Italy in the late 1960's and told me about her findings and her work in preserving these dances. I later received a book with her notes and cassette tape in the mail from her to begin expanding my dance repertoire. She admired my tenacity of working on this preservation project and wanted to support my journey. I guess my research in college was foreshadowing what was to come of my dance career.

I only spoke with her a few more times after that initial phone call. After she passed away in 2003, I was compelled to keep preserving to not let her hard work be for nothing. She was proud of my work and loved that I started my company to perform these dances. I shared with her my dreams and told her I would carry on what she started. She encouraged me with a few simple words: if I follow my passion then my heart will not be disappointed. She was right. No regrets if you follow your heart.

La Furlana is an elegant, waltz inspired dance with a 3/4 tempo where the dance begins with the man on one side and the women on the opposite side facing each other with a bit of space between them. They travel towards each other using waltz movements of down, up, up by bending the knee with the first foot flat on the floor and then taking two steps on the ball of the foot completing the waltz timing. The couple arrives face to face after a few waltz steps.

At that moment, the woman, who has a scarf attached to her skirt by softly tucking it into the top of her waist, hands her partner the other end of the scarf for him to hold. I believe this is the most romantic part of the dance. The moment they meet, she softly hands him this scarf which connects the two of them together. It might make a perfect proposal dance. Picturing this moment where he pops the question to his partner. The scarf represents their communication line from her heart to his.

What are their hearts saying to each other? They maintain eye contact throughout the entire dance as they never face away from each other unless they are turning. Continuous contact visually is rare these days with technology. It's so refreshing to perform this dance for this exact reason.

Throughout the dance, the couple travel by tracing a large circular pattern with waltz steps as well as some steps that sway from side to side. When they are traveling throughout the space, his steps move forward while she travels backwards. In the peak of the dance, you will find the woman pauses to roll in and out of her partner's arms, by enveloping herself into the scarf and then unwinding to release. His fingers hold one end of the scarf while she rolls in and out holding the other end.

They only touch via the scarf, which I found interesting since many of the folk dances connect usually by one hand or at the crease of the elbow to hook for a do-si-do.

This absence of touch contains a sweetness and innocence factor. While the waltz steps hold an elegant yet flirtatious quality, the turning and traveling are playful as the couple glide across the floor. When you hear the melody of the mandolin, it sets the tone of the dance. Another romantic moment in the dance is when the woman is lassoed by her partner with the scarf around her lower back and waist while they perform a perfect box step in sync. There are a few slight variations of this same dance. I admired this version for the soft, circular floor pattern it traces throughout the space, the additional element of a scarf and the absence of touch.

Personally, I see La Furlana as a whisper of Venetian life. The sway of the gondolas is reflected in the swaying waltz steps. The romantic moments of being close to your love when your heart is captured by the scarf. Suddenly you find yourself in sync with them like two hearts beating as one. Demonstrating the softest of movements can still be powerful. This is what I acquired from learning this dance. Love is powerful even when you can't touch it. For me, the scarf represents the connection between us all as humans around the world. One thread connects us all. We all seek to be loved and hopefully waltz our way a little closer to the one we cherish.

Being a light-hearted number, it has easily become a favorite of my dancers over the years. It certainly shows a softer side of Italian dances and creates a lighter mood on stage. Once I was comfortable with the choreography, I added Venetian masks for the dancers to wear. The masks enhanced the mysteriousness of the dancers as if they were meeting for the first time at Carnevale in Venice. Creating a bit of mystery keeps the allure alive. What's behind the mask? I hope it's love.

Mi amor, we must buy another train ticket as we continue on to Florence. The next chapter brings to light an important woman that played a major role in dance history.

5,6,7,8

- Do you have a special tradition that you and your parent(s) share?
- Do you wear an invisible mask in life? If so, why?
- What did you learn on your last trip?
- Do you have a fear that you have worked through?

A unique perspective from the
Ponte Vecchio bridge in Florence.

Florence

A mere two-hour train ride away from Venice is where you will find an explosion of art and science. I look forward to feasting on the scenery as I approach the city. My desire is to spend more time in Florence to learn and explore but is diminished by the crowded tourist-filled streets. Every tour of Italy stops in the jewel of Tuscany and for good reason. Discovering new museums or acquiring a deeper comprehension of history with each visit, keeps my lantern of curiosity burning. A city where the birthplace of the Renaissance curates the works of Leonardo Da Vinci, Michelangelo, along with a long list of extraordinary creations, makes anyone marvel.

Being the epicenter of the boom of the Renaissance era, this flowering city was the host to the most spectacular art, science and innovation. Seeing Michelangelo's David statue, the Ponte Vecchio bridge or simply tasting some of the best gelato makes enduring the crowds worth it. These are just a handful of reasons why I circle back to this city whenever I am traveling north.

My repeated excursions have enabled me to become familiar with how to get around. This would be my third time in this beautiful city. As a young girl, I enjoyed seeing where *Pinnochio* originated. As a young woman, my dancers and I were inspired by the many buskers on the streets showing off their skills by playing an instrument or painted up as a statue. With each expedition, my itinerary contains historic landmarks to admire and activities to fill my creative soul. Seeing these cities at different stages in my life gives me perspective and a profound appreciation of my heritage. But this time, the visit was just for Greg and me.

Greg and I decided to take a day trip by taking the train from Rome which is a ninety-minute ride. Traveling by train is comfortable and relaxing. I couldn't wait to explore this city again with my husband by my side. His thirst for history and science will both be quenched. We started with the Uffizi Gallery which is my must-see museum in Florence. The lines are almost always long to enter, but shortly after we joined the queue, we signed up for a tour. Joining the tour with a guide was no more than the price of admission. We booked our entry time which gave us about two hours to spend elsewhere. This is my recommendation to never wait in any line, book early or get a tour so you don't waste time standing in line. This saves you time and money. Surrounding the museum is quite an impressive display with over two dozen statues of various figures configured in a U-shaped portico. With Galileo, Machiavelli and Da Vinci all peering down, I was reminded of all their accomplishments. Plus, a smattering of artisans are usually selling their wares close by to peruse.

Unbeknownst to the usual traveler, there is a secret passageway called Vasari's Corridor built high above. The passageway travels from the Palazzo Vecchio, through the Uffizi Gallery, over the Ponte Vecchio, over part of a church, and landing into the Boboli Gardens, where the duke lived with his family. This secret walkway was commissioned by Grand Duke Cosimo I in 1564. It's nearly impossible to go through this corridor today without special permission and an Uffizi guard.

How cool would it be to walk through that passageway!

After capturing a few photos there in the gallery, we wandered a little further away from the crowds to browse on the chance to see locals at work. With the Arno River in the background, we ventured across the Ponte Vecchio, or the old bridge. The Ponte Vecchio today accommodates only jewelers due to a law passed by Ferdinand de' Medici in 1593. He didn't appreciate the aroma coming from the previous owners nor their goods. Countless memories of walking across this bridge come to mind because of its beauty and grandeur.

Like a moth to a flame, I tugged on Greg's arm and pointed to enter this beautiful jewelry store. Florence is known for goldsmith work dating back to the Etruscan age. Their work gained the respect of royalty, since they created works of art that evoked emotions, much like dancers. Echoing the family affair that continues this line of work, a father passes his profession onto his son or daughter as they mold and shape the metals with such confidence. My eyes scrolled through the cases that were filled with rubies, gold topaz and other jewels that were added to produce exquisite pieces. The works they create are inspired by historical paintings combined with fresh ideas to fabricate original and contemporary work. I pictured ancestors dancing while adorned with precious stones.

One of the staff spoke with me about the process. Heating a gold plate and then cooling it off quickly is first. Then, they give it shape and etch a pattern on it. Finally, they separate it into parts and combine it with a bit of polish. The final product is incredible whether it is tools, jewelry or decor for your home. It was enthralling to see all the products they had to offer. I thought about all the tools my father kept in his box and how he showed me how to use them all as things needed to be fixed. While I did not take up my father's profession, I admired seeing families work together to share one passion. I regretted not having more room in my luggage for some home décor. Next time for sure!

Filled with a variety of establishments, the city seems to welcome us to experience it all. From jewelry to art and everything in between one can fill their time and luggage easily here. As we proceed further, I pointed out a few inspirational statues and details that were used as my muse for modern pieces with my dancers. How can you not be wrapped up in a city that blooms literally and figuratively with beauty.

Gaining more miles on our shoes, we came upon a butcher shop, where they believe that carne or meat, is king. Greg was salivating at the window. No parts of the animal are ever wasted with any of the delicious dishes that are served. Many of the butchers are part of a long line of family members that took up this profession. Another generational job that is passed down to the next to observe, practice and then manage the business. Stopping to rest a bit, we watched the butcher carve up a large piece of meat with skillful precision. The animals are raised in beautiful pastures with free spaces to roam feeding on plentiful grains. As delicious as it looked, we resisted and kept on walking with our eyes on the time. Missing our appointment to see the museum would be a disaster since this was just a day jaunt.

With a few minutes to spare, we grabbed a small bite of fresh bread and cheese and headed back to the museum. We were met by our tour guide to begin our tour inside. Uffizi means offices and this building was used as the offices for the powerful Medici family of Florence. It contains forty-five rooms featuring thousands of works of precious art by various painters and sculptures. Besides self-portraits and statues, it showcases much of the Medici family collection of jewels, medallions and scientific instruments.

The Medici made their money through banking and commerce and were able to fund the most famous artists of the Renaissance. From Bottecelli's soft colored Birth of Venus to the sculpture of Ariadne asleep, there is something for everyone in this museum of greatness. Lorenzo the Magnificent, Cosmo, and many other family members are also featured in some of the most striking art around the city and are highlighted in the gallery. But the most fascinating Medici family member to me is Catherine. Not surprisingly known to the world as Catherine the Great. I relished in seeing her family portraits and any artifacts that related to her.

Born in Florence, Italy in 1519, Catherine would follow in her family's tradition of being a patron of the arts. Both of her parents died when she was an infant, so she was then raised by her extended family, mostly by her grandmother. She had a love for fashion, architecture and the arts. This struck a chord with me, and I was in the right city to see her life up close and personal.

Married to Henry II, they held a lavish wedding that entailed music, poetry and dance. She became the Queen of France and over the years, they had ten children. Yes ten! My maternal grandmother had nine children. I can hardly keep up with having eight to twelve dancers on tour. I am impressed with how families take care of this many children. She must have been exhausted and overwhelmed to say the least. What a huge amount of responsibility to oversee that many people!

Queen Catherine moved with her husband from Florence, Italy to France. During this time period, France endured several religious wars between the Catholics and Protestants. Catherine tried various tactics to bring peace, but nothing seemed to work. Ballet seemed to be the course of action she chose for political statements. She invented the ballet de cour, where kings, queens, and courtiers performed to an adoring public. From learning about her in college as a dance major, being here was like seeing my dance history come to life.

Her family was known for being a huge source of funds for artists of all kinds. Hiring artists to create work or to entertain for extraordinary events and parties. Catherine wanted to bring a new style of dance called ballet from Italy to France. Balletto, meaning little dance, in Italian was a way for everyone to learn the proper forms of behavior. Ballet classes taught a person how to eloquently move and act to be in the court. One would learn the proper etiquette to greet one another, how to bow and hold postures while dancing. This training became essential to all men especially.

My, how times have changed!

Ballet became part of the acting with poetry and later scenic design. The first ballet was called *Ballet de comedic* in 1581. The themes of these productions took on myths of queen goddesses turning men into beasts. This was reflecting the wars that were going on around them. Life is always reflected in art in some manner. This time period was no different than today. If it wasn't for her support, I am not sure ballet would exist.

The choreography for these ballets took on more organizational patterns. Lines, squares or diamonds were the formations of choice for choreography. Their steps were calculated and precise where no one was out of line or step. They took their practices seriously. These patterns and moves reflected their higher power, their wealth, and their innovation, especially with the elaborate scene designs to help tell the story. I could only dream of having that large of a budget to put on productions.

Cha-Ching!

In the past, their costumes were made with lighter fabrics, like silk, used to see the flow and features of the body lines. Because of her great taste for fashion and being short like myself, Catherine brought attention to the invention of a higher heel. She had a pair made for her wedding to stand a little taller. These shoes created a lift and grand stature with their moves as they danced. Who doesn't want to look their best when you are in the line of the court? With her endless funding, she also had the folding fan, handkerchiefs and ladies' drawers made. On top of those items, she brought into vogue the use of makeup and perfume as well as hair pieces and dyes. *Grazie* Catherine! All these items my company uses today at every show minus the perfume. However, after a show a quick spritz is needed!

The masters of the Renaissance are all on display at the Uffizi. Rafael, Michelangelo, and Leonardo da Vinci are the standout featured artists. Hours go by like minutes, as we move from room to room being captivated by the art. Greg seeing details that I didn't catch and I sharing a creative spin to what it might mean, we exchange ideas in each room. A theme caught my eye in a few of the paintings. The use of light and dark were the most intriguing to me. I see this shading method repeated in many of the arts from ballet to music. Life has both light and dark moments, I guess that is why it resonates with me and others so well.

As a choreographer, directing the audience where to look helps tell the story of the dance. These artists found a way with color to draw my attention and seemingly light up the main characters on the canvas. Shading certain parts of the piece and leaving space in others offers balance. This can be approached in dance with movement as well as lighting or staging.

I tend to ask myself: *Where is the focus in the dance? Is the focus on center stage or on a certain dancer playing a role? Does the dance have a focal point on stage where the dancer returns to in order to make a statement?*

King Louis XIV stood center stage portraying the Sun King in a ballet. He was the focal point and wanted his entire court to know that everything revolved around him. Being strategically placed center stage set the tone and attitude for the dance. He was standing in the light while all the other characters were in the shadows.

Organizing where the dancers look, throughout the piece, is another example of how to use focus. By adjusting the head position or eyes to face a different direction can suggest a completely different thought. If King Louis stood to one side of the stage instead of center, would it be as majestic or powerful? No, the placement of him being center stage is striking. When looking at a painting, your eyes are drawn to the center unless the artist shows you where to look. As artists, we guide the audience to share our thoughts or story.

After making a phrase of movement, I comb through it again to detail where the focal point is for every move. Dancers could begin a piece with their backs to the audience or all facing a corner of the stage to make the audience look in that direction. Finding unique ways to change the focus or staying consistent allows the story to remain clear. This mirrors a bit of life, doesn't it? Finding the main point and adjusting it from time to time allows us to stay on track and find a clear path to our goal. Another life lesson is to know your goals but understand you can adjust them in life.

Northern folk dances have a clear intent that comes naturally. A dancer will lock eyes with their partner and remain fixed on them for most of the dance. When a dance calls for changing partners throughout the piece, one must instantly shift their attention on the next step to make that transition smooth and seamless. This fascinates me since I don't know of too many other professions that look at their co-workers in the eye that long.

Imagine a group of dancers looking in all different directions. This would seem chaotic and without any organization at all. If the piece is about chaos, then that would be a perfect way to show it. Now think about a group of dancers all looking in the same direction. This has a different connotation and feeling. It shows organization, unity, control and perhaps power. Finally, what if the entire group looked in the direction of the audience? How would that look and feel for both the dancers and the audience? The audience may feel like they are a part of the dance, or they may feel like they are going to be attacked especially if the dancers were in a line coming straight towards them.

What if Leonardo Da Vinci changed the focus of where Mona Lisa was looking? Would it be as famous? Focus matters greatly in life as well as the arts.

The Medici family concentrated on how they could exclude themselves from the rest, using their power and wealth for all sorts of innovations. Building the secret passageway so as not to walk amongst the people or hiring artists to perform for their lavish parties separated the Medici family from the commoners. This exclusivity way of thinking began to manifest in all facets of life. They revered themselves above the commoners like a higher power.

So much of the art we saw in Florence was a retelling of biblical stories or religiously inspired. I can see why, knowing the Medici family produced several popes! So perhaps, the portraying the divine within the art that they commissioned helped nurture the image that the family had been blessed by God. It was fascinating to experience the city that this family molded.

Tresso

When discussing the flowering city of Florence, a dance from the Tuscany region I learned from Federica comes to mind. Tresso is a lively dance with a 2/4 rhythm performed by three couples in a line one behind the other usually starting at one corner of the room or stage. Each couple is in the closed hold position ballroom style when performing these steps. The man offers his left hand to the woman and places his right hand on her waist. She holds his left hand with her right hand and places her left hand on his shoulder. The couples remain in this closed position throughout the entire dance.

The couples perform three different movements throughout this dance. The first step is called gallop where one foot chases the other placing your weight on the balls of your feet. The second step to know is a step ball-change step where the feet do a quick transfer of weight from side to side. These are small steps that stay underneath the body to perform quickly. The final step to use in the dance is the step hop step. All three of these steps are repeated throughout this dance.

This brightly spirited dance has a weaving pattern like a braid where the lead couple weaves in and out of the other two couples creating a figure eight pattern. They use the gallop step to weave in front of the next couple and behind the third couple. Only one couple at a time starts this weaving so that there is consistency and organization to the dance. While the lead couple is weaving in and out the other two couples perform the step ball-change step in place. Each couple gets a turn at this braid pattern. Once that is complete, the dancers use the step hop step to rotate as a couple. Braiding as a couple is fun to experience and keeps the mind engaged the entire time since you are navigating in and out of the other couples dancing.

At the end of the sequence of movements, the dance repeats from the beginning once more to find all three couples forming a circle. In the circle formation the use of the step ball-change and step hop step is used. To me this ending formation looked like a flower or three-leaf clover since there are three couples for this dance. Seeing the couples rotate in this formation is like watching a flower bloom.

Dances like this one were performed in the 15th century for various celebrations, festivals and weddings. Other festive occasions included visits from kings and ambassadors, military victories or lavish banquets. Dance was training to learn refinement, good manners, and modesty.

No need to gallop, we can walk with proper posture back to the train station now. My quest continues in the next chapter as I venture to Bologna with my husband. We encounter medieval castles and a better awareness of the human body from the inside out.

5,6,7,8

- What would your family legacy be?
- If you sculpted a piece of art that reflected you, what would it look like?
- Is there a profession in your family that has been passed down? If so, what profession?
- How do you find focus in life?

Towers in Bologna

Bologna

Venturing to a new stop on our tour, Greg and I decided to stay in the city of Bologna. A train from Florence to Bologna is less than an hour. Peering out the window during the ride, I was excited to put another pin on my map. Extending from the Apennine Mountains to the Po River, this Emilia-Romagna region is known for its medieval cities, balsamic vinegar and seaside resorts. I just kept picturing Rapunzel letting her hair down from the window of a castle.

We exited the train toting our bags and circled the block to find our hotel, which was right across from the train station. Our tired and weary bodies were so confused, we missed it completely the first time around the block. Arriving at the hotel door, we were greeted and checked in. After a brief nap and some delicious food, we couldn't wait to devour this medieval masterpiece. We were only staying a few days, so we wanted to do as much as possible.

A handful of steps from our hotel, the Porta Galliera, a structural gate from the former medieval walls, welcomed us. Looking to my right, a long portico of boutiques and cafes awaited us to explore. My inner fashionista sense gave me that tingling feeling that this was going to be a great city for us. We stayed between the Centro Storico area and the train station, where everything we needed was at our fingertips.

After a five-minute walk stood two towers or *Le due torri* that are sure to be admired by any visitor. There are 498 steps on a steep wooden staircase. We didn't feel the need to climb to the top, but rather admired them from below. The names of the two towers are Asinelli Tower which stands about 319 feet tall and Garisenda Tower at 200 feet tall. From my perspective below, they looked enormous. They are named after families which had them constructed between the years of 1109 and 1119. These medieval towers represent the strength and power of the local families.

Greg, the history buff he is, found a printing shop opened in 1633 to create printed fabrics is still open today. The large machine, invented to help with this process, smoothed out the fabrics then stamped them with paints to create a pattern. This machine was refined by none other than Leonardo Da Vinci. Leonardo, a true Renaissance man, had both artist and inventor on his resume for sure. These two qualities help Greg and I work well together. He, the scientist, and I, the creative artist, saw these beautiful, printed fabrics everywhere being sold. Some were hand embroidered and others featured unique patterns of color. The shop still uses this invention to create beautiful quality products. I am told it takes hours to produce one tablecloth. This takes real dedication and patience. I appreciated the time each product demands because I do the same with each dance I preserve or choreography I create. These precious fabrics, bought for special occasions in the Renaissance period, were popular because the embroidery wasn't affordable in the rural areas.

Our next destination was the famous fountain of Neptune, god of the sea. As we explored the Piazza Maggiore, my glamour goddess was called by the window displays along the way. We leisurely strolled along Independence Street under the porticoes seeking more treasures to add to our collection. Each store had its own charm and flair. I acquired a couple of elegant tops to wear for special occasions. There were pasta-makers, churches, banks, and bakers. We kept crossing and recrossing the street to see what was on the other side. Our path was like a zigzag stitching seam. My favorite purchase was a bright true red blouse that was off the shoulder with ruffles all around the neckline. It was a perfect top for our evening dinner. None of the prices seemed outrageous, nothing like the Prada and Gucci stores in Florence. A square white purse completed my ensemble. This leather purse with a smile-shaped zipper had me at *ciao*! I couldn't wait to wear it as a cross-body the next day.

We were on a shopping lottery, checking off many boxes on our wish list. Next on the list, spices! We stopped in front of a spice and oil store that emitted an incredible aroma. Our noses led us inside to add a new spice to our collection. We needed to find local anise seed to bring back to my family for baking Easter bread. This is a complicated spice to find in pure seed form. But luckily, I was able to stock up for the holidays. Greg also chose a few olive oils to dip with fresh bread and of course some wine for later. These kinds of experiences immerse me into the region. Tasting the bread, local wine, local seasonings are all pieces of the puzzle that are found in each dance I find.

With bags of our shopping finds in hand, we finally made it to the fountain of Neptune which was magnificent. However, it happened to be under restoration during our visit. Even covered with scaffolding, the face of the god of the sea was still visible, and almost looked like he was peering down at us from a hole in the wood and pipes. Yikes! The statue, even encased, had so much movement. Swinging his arms, while holding his iconic trident, Neptune isn't satisfied at the top of the structure. He still has somewhere else more pressing to be. His fluid shape, ripped abs and structure said it all.

Hearing the roar of our stomachs, we decided to find a place to enjoy some Bolognese sauce. Each restaurant or cozy cafe we passed, my mouth watered with anticipation. Bologna doesn't disappoint as a culinary capital. Many of our Italian beloved dishes hail from this area, like the Bolognese sauce. We found a great place to rest our feet and enjoy a pasta dinner. The bright flavors of a marinara sauce with tomatoes, garlic, basil, onions mixed with oil and seasonings hit the spot with just the right amount of salt and pepper. We savored each bite and wiped our plates clean.

Each region of Italy offers a different palate of delights for my tongue to try. I tend to avoid meat sauces on my pasta in the States, because I find them too greasy and lack the depth of flavor the marinara should have. However, this Bolognese sauce we had that day was nothing like I expected. It had a creaminess and heartiness to it yet maintained all the palpable flavors. The atmosphere didn't hurt our experience either. We dined al fresco and watched all the people sightseeing, shopping and enjoying the day, just as we had done. We were in no hurry and continued sipping our wine as we watched the evening sky take over. These experiences are worth recreating at home when we have great meals, sip our drinks and share the adventures of our day.

It's easy to find fresh, high-quality ingredients, even in the heart of the city, which make farm to table meals possible. The simple recipes in the local dishes allow the spices to shine here in Bologna. This is a great tip for any new cook. Keep it simple, use fresh ingredients and add spices and herbs more often.

Pasta is very easy to make and share. The simplicity is what made it popular for everyone to enjoy over the centuries. Mix the flour, shape it into a pile and place an egg in the center of your volcano of flour, or add water instead of an egg. Hand mix the ingredients and start rolling it out.

There was something mesmerizing about the way my grandmother used the heel of her hand to press the dough forward. Her hands created fancy choreography. As a child, I sat up on a chair watching her work the dough. She taught me how to mix by placing her hands on top of mine. Then roll out the dough with a rolling pin. These are some of the unforgettable memories I hold dear. Teaching a child to cook with just a few ingredients is a life survival skill. Making numerous recipes with family over the years was like attending an Italian culinary school. No one ever goes hungry at an Italian's house. NO ONE. It is just our way of sharing a bit of ourselves with others. We will feed anyone. And making different pasta shapes was part of the fun.

Have you ever seen the birth of Venus painting? Well, Venus, the goddess of love and desire, is the inspiration for the shape of the pasta tortellini. According to the locals, the Salt Legend has it that Venus's navel caught an innkeeper's eye and so he dashed to his kitchen to create an egg pasta inspired by the goddess's belly button. Crazy right? Inspiration is unpredictable when it hits you in the face. Or in this case in the belly! After I heard that, all I could do was stare at the tortellini on my plate as a group of belly buttons. Of course, I ate it anyway. It was delicious, but it made me giggle.

Cooking together breathes life into any family. Kitchen counters become the stage where memories and traditions come to shine. Why not explore the vast variety of shapes dough can take on. There are hundreds of shapes of pasta that can be formed with just your fingers. Expanding my skills, I continued to take on different pasta dishes. My first taste of independence was measuring the flour and cracking the egg in the center, shaping the dough and boiling my creation. Empowered and confident to do more activities, pasta making was a triumphant event for me. Having my family surrounding me to assist along the way to achieve small goals, like mixing dough, has helped me to this day achieve more than I could dream. They provided the encouragement necessary to continue trying and learning new skills on my own.

Speaking of expanding my education, I simply couldn't be this close to possibly the oldest university in the world and not visit for a day. We didn't know much about the University of Bologna other than it was established in 1088 AD. That's not a typo. One Thousand, Eighty-eight. That is over 700 years before Giuseppe Garibaldi united Italy, still 200 years before Marco Polo traveled to Asia on the silk road and even a decade earlier than the start of the first crusade.

Luckily for us, there are some museums on the campus. One of them was dedicated to the work the university collected for hundreds of years studying anatomy. It was the stuff of horrors initially, with body parts preserved floating in different sized glass jars. In an instant, curiosity overtakes feelings of repulsiveness. Since I recently studied anatomy again for my certifications with Pilates and yoga, I was intrigued. Most of my anatomy knowledge remains from my college days, taking numerous trips to the cadaver lab as a dance major. We observed different levels of muscle development and the effects of smoking on the body. One of my fellow dance majors quit smoking the day after we saw what years of smoking does to all aspects of the human body. The gray and discolored muscles of smokers came back to me as I examined the old jars. Even though this was science based, Greg was not a fan of looking at muscles and jars filled with fluids. I, on the other hand, leveled up my interest in muscles in motion.

My mind boggled to imagine the beginnings of anatomy studies. Picturing the foot, the tendons, and ligaments connecting with all the muscles and bones in such a way to allow movement and balance is mind-blowing. Range of motion is always a consideration for my yoga practice and how it can be enhanced. Working through different poses and flows increases flexibility for myself or a client is a goal. If a client is possibly recuperating from an injury, I usually say after ten sessions I feel a difference, after ten more, I notice a difference and after an additional ten, one might expect others to notice a difference. Progress can be slow but rewarding.

As a dancer, I have had to specifically develop my feet by strengthening my arch and working the dexterity in my toes. An exercise that helps is to spread the toes and move each one individually or use the foot to pick up a towel. Greg, by contrast, is limited to one foot motion. He shakes his head at my foot strength. No matter what his intention, it just looks like he is slightly curling his toes. The feet must articulate to the fullest extent when we dance, no matter what style.

When I studied traditional Indian dance, the teacher showed us intricate finger positions that reflected specific animals. Some of my dancers didn't have the finger dexterity to master those positions. The way those movements are performed, and how they are improved over time can differ from person to person. These were some of the questions the curious minds at the University of Bologna began answering almost a millennia ago through the study of anatomy. After going through the museum, I was in awe of the details and history of the human body. Filling my brain with more data pushes me to never stop learning.

From learning more about the mind and body, it was time to work on the spirit. On our last day in Bologna, we took the day to go to the seven churches of Saint Stefano. A seven-minute walk from Neptune, the cobblestone pathway led us to the seven churches and the Basilica of Santo Stefano dating back to the seventh century! A quiet piazza with visual scars of its past is surrounded by a complex of buildings. San Petronio is one of the patron saints of Bologna and the seven churches are dedicated to him. Warm light filters through the windows of each holy space along with symbols, statues, and charming courtyards. Spending a whole afternoon here painted a clear picture of what the dances of this region should feel like: regal, spiritual and enchanting.

Enveloped by the holy architecture, we visited four churches to light a candle and say a prayer. A traveling tradition is to attend a mass and light a candle to honor those loved ones that have passed on. A simple gesture brings a bit of peace and an opportunity to include my family on my journey. It brings me comfort to think they travel with me in spirit and offer guidance when I am struggling to find my way in life. It was a peaceful afternoon to reflect.

Admiring the area, I found a quiet space to be the backdrop for a video. Greg counts me down and says "Action!" I recorded a message to announce the upcoming dance tour which included dances from this region. Capturing photos and videos from the different cities to incorporate into my classes and speaking engagements gives students a broader perspective of the region. Anytime I can include photos and videos makes it a well-rounded presentation.

When we dance, we speak, echoes in my mind.

When we dance, we speak. Whenever I give a workshop or a lecture demonstration, I use this phrase to emphasize how dance is used to communicate. Often, it's very literal, a touchdown dance is a celebration, a couple's first wedding dance shows their love and devotion to one another. There are specific gestures with meanings throughout a ballet piece, like rolling hands upward to mean "let's dance" or pointing to the ring finger for marriage. Not dancing is also communicating a message. A girl at a school dance may not be participating because she is shy or doesn't like the boy she is paired with as her partner. We are always communicating through movement or the lack of it.

The phrase children should be seen and not heard is a good illustration of this. It's not that children should not be included in the adult events, by contrast, the first part says that they should be seen. Not heard however, is referring to how and what they communicate. Being quiet, respectful, are demonstrated through their movements and reflect they are well behaved. We have all witnessed a child remain quiet, but still earn a scolding from their parents for rolling eyes or turning away.

So, when we dance, what are we communicating? When participating in a court dance, from a region in northern Italy, I think about what they are expressing. What were the participants communicating back then? Were they making a political statement? Were they showing off new innovative moves? Or were they demonstrating strength? This is why it is imperative I stand in different regions of Italy to use all my senses to absorb their messages of centuries ago.

Obviously, everyone enjoys learning some steps at a renaissance festival, where my lord and my lady can pretend to be French nobility and mimic the traditions of a long ago past. People make mistakes, go left instead of right, and chuckle a bit because it isn't seen as anything serious. They are just having fun! It's not like their livelihood depends on their dancing.

But, what if it did? And what if it was serious? Imagine being a merchant in a 17th century French court. You are being judged almost solely on showing proper respect for all your various dance partners, or perhaps judged on how well your movements blended with the group. Your position in society was for one of the first times in history not fixed, but it was marked by how far away from the duke or king you were within the court dances. How you performed in the grand ballroom dictated that distance and was the difference between favorable trade charters or possibly higher taxes.

Dance for them was now much more associated with work and less fun, I would imagine. Like those children, to receive praise you are seen and not heard, but still through movement communicating respect, order and allegiance to the hierarchy. The fun-loving lord and lady, giggling and tripping, are viewed as incompetent, not whimsical, especially when the king of France is the most prolific dancer in the room.

When we dance, we speak. From this perspective, it is easy to see how, rather than blunder or rely on their own skill, a wealthier merchant could employ a more skilled dancer to represent him. A class of performers come to replace the members of the court. An audience is born along with ballet. Vastly different from the outer circle of people waiting for their turn in the middle of a southern Italian folk dance. This audience now permanently watches and acknowledges the individual performances they approve of, helping the monarch decide what or more concisely who to feature and who is relegated to smaller and more minor parts.

As we take our final bow to Bologna, I know we will return someday to step back in time to the medieval period, to dance, to pray and expand our minds.

Giga Emiliana

This dance hails from the Emilia-Romagna region. It was the first dance Federica taught us at the conference. My company has been performing it for over twenty years. It is a favorite of the dancers and audiences alike.

It begins with men and women partnered up in a line with one couple behind the next. The man leads his lady into a circle by walking. The music will then begin to pick up in tempo and the man performs a sliding or chasing movement forward while the lady does the same movement facing him and backwards. The couple grasps both hands while doing a step ball change step side to side which goes into a do-si-do embracing each other around the waist with one arm. All couples take four steps forward towards the center and then turn to walk four steps out from the center of the circle. The man will then hold up one arm gesturing for his lady to spin like an arch turn in ballroom dance. This sequence of movements repeats several times allowing all couples to find their stride and refine their footing. After a few rounds there is a distinct music change which signals the dancers to form two single file lines with the men on one side and the women on the other. One couple at a time holding both hands slide down the center of the aisle and jumps back in line to wait for the next couple to do the same. As the last couple slides down the aisle, the process repeats but this time each couple does a polka step in a closed hold position and dances to their final spot on the floor. The music takes a coda while each couple finds a final pose to strike.

Every time my company has performed this dance it brings so many joyous smiles immediately from the start. What a great feeling to look your partner in the eyes for most of the dance and feed off each other's energy to move continuously. From the start of the chasing movement there is a spark of energy that strikes and just becomes a flame as the choreography continues. The tunnel formation near the end of the dance reminds me of when I learned the stroll where you make an aisle and two at a time groove down the center and show off their best moves. But, in this case you did a polka step or a gallop down the center with your partner in a closed hold position or just a two-hand hold. This dance taught me how to connect with a partner for an entire dance. This constant connection can be a life lesson in life. We go through life and sometimes lose touch with those we adore. This dance gives you a big reminder that it's nice to stay in touch and see what can be accomplished when you work together.

Hand in hand we leave the castles of Bologna behind and head for the eternal city. The next chapter is where we catch up with an old friend from Rome who gives us a personal tour of ruins. We also tell a dramatic story to the end of our quest in Italy.

5,6,7,8

- What do you cook with your family?
- Do you visit new cities? If so, where did you go?
- What message do you communicate without saying a word?
- What activities help you expand your knowledge?

The view of Roman ruins with the
Colosseum in the background.

Rome

Rain.

On our first full day in Rome, we made plans to meet my friend, Valerio, for a tour of the city. It is early May, and the rain is pouring down. We have no umbrella. The forecast says that the rain will let up at any moment, but right now, we have finished our breakfast of pastries and espresso, and are ready to battle through the rain. We hustle to the ATM to get cash, street to street, portico to roof covering, all the way to the metro station, already running behind schedule. At every corner, an immigrant merchant is pushing overpriced umbrellas on us. We have faith the weather will turn, and luckily my friend Valerio also had faith in us. It was a rough start to the morning, and we arrived at the Colosseo metro stop much later than we had anticipated. I hate being late, but we were doing our best.

I knew Valerio when he was a high school student. He participated in a foreign exchange program that brought him from Roma, Italy to my humble West Virginia hometown. I taught at the school he was attending, and my dance studio became a hub for many of the foreign exchange students at the time. They were like family. I learned more from those students than I probably taught them.

Whenever I come across a foreign exchange student, I love getting to know them. It's a way for me to travel to their country without getting on a plane. One girl was from Thailand. She taught me her traditional dances from home. What a joy and gift to see and hear about these dances! Her movements were beautiful and controlled. Unlike my hair in this rain! While I look like Sofia Loren with an Italian scarf on my head, I'm no movie star.

Valerio wanted to show us the Colosseum and the Forum. His eagerness to be our tour guide that day was delightful and heartfelt. He was now a young man compared to the scrawny high school kid I remembered. He was well dressed with khaki pants, and a sharp blue blazer. We dressed a little more relaxed. Greg wore a college shirt, and I was inventing an athleisure look with my casual dance wear vibe. At the time, Valerio was finishing medical school as an ear, nose and throat doctor. Seeing him accomplishing his goals filled me with pride. To reconnect with these students rekindles my fire to keep learning. It is during this incredible vacation when I will meet my dance instructor Chiara from Naples.

The rain had stopped, but the gray sky lingered as we headed for the Colosseum. Valerio explained that there was a charge for the enormous, ancient stadium, but after that it was free to walk around the Forum and the Arch of Titus. The line was short that day, probably because of the weather, so we got right in. Some rainy days are worth it to venture out.

There were guided tours available, but Valerio, a native Roman, would provide us all the details we needed and more. It was interesting to hear the history from a real Roman. The emperor Vespasian began constructing the massive stadium, known as the Flavian Amphitheater, in 79 AD. It took almost a decade to build and could seat around 70,000 people. That is more than the population of my hometown! The corridors were lined with exhibits like a museum. There was so much history to learn and different displays to pursue.

We enjoyed looking at different gladiatorial costumes. Greg hates when I call them costumes, but this is what they are. The armor and weapons the gladiators used were forged to mimic the types of weapons warriors used that the Roman army had already vanquished. The Samnite, or Secutor, armor and weapons were fashioned after the warriors of Abruzzo and Campania regions of Italy. Those regions were conquered hundreds of years earlier and already a part of the Roman Empire when the gladiators were fighting in the Colosseum. The gladiators of Imperial Rome could be volunteers or slaves from all throughout the Empire, mimicking this specific style of fighting. Hence, their armor and weapons were costumes in a performance. And what a performance they had in those days!

The power and spectacle of each event brought out so many Romans to witness. Valerio explained the different Roman periods. As I gazed intensely at the Roman garb, I was imagining what those days were like. In addition to the gladiatorial displays, there were Roman legionnaire uniforms from different periods on display as we rounded the various levels of the stadium. The gladiators trained for hours every day to prepare for their performance. They fought with shields and weapons, but generally did not wear layers of heavy armor for protection as the legionaries would. I can picture in my mind the sole gladiator, thrusting and parrying for hours rehearsing his possible improvisation choreography, ready to react to whatever moves his opponent may deploy.

Rehearsals for dancers can be exhausting, but it's important to rehearse often on your own. Some dancers tend to wait until a group rehearsal to review the information. I witnessed this fatal mistake quite a bit. My advice to them is to take a few minutes every day to go over their solo or group dance. Making sure to thoroughly know their part will allow more time at the group rehearsal to go over spacing and other issues.

Being consistent with rehearsals helps muscle memory kick in and calms the nervousness on stage. The body will remember what comes next if you rehearse it frequently, a method that I am sure the gladiators used. Over the years, I made rehearsing my solo a part of my daily workout to keep my cardio capabilities fresh. It becomes second nature to execute the order of moves or react immediately to a partner's actions. As a bonus, all this repetition supports your stamina. With the folk dances being of high energy, we rely on endurance. No dancer wants to feel or look winded on stage. I would assume that an exhausted gladiator would also be a losing gladiator. Keeping up your strength and staying alert also keeps you alive in any arena.

Besides stamina, we need flexibility. My morning yoga practice on the day of my performance helps me to stretch and release anything that was in the past. The mind can begin racing on performance day with thoughts of what can go wrong. Yoga can calm the mind and body and put those thoughts to bed. Once we arrive at a venue, the dancers set aside time to stretch backstage right before we go on. Stretching major muscles such as your legs and back to get warm before we go full out on stage prevents injury.

These dances that we perform are not for the weakest of hearts, that's for sure! Many of the folk dances we endure are done with a 6/8 tempo and have intricate fast footwork. Therefore, it's important to train in our off season. Do dancers have an off season? No. Even though we are not on tour, we are still training and caring for our bodies. My company also performs other styles as well like jazz, modern, and even ballroom in our one hour showcases. Cross training with these other styles can enhance our cardio capabilities. One way I bump up my game is to play a favorite song and start moving to the entire song. Then, if that seems easy, I go for two songs or more. Slowly, I am building up my cardio with a playlist that motivates me. Strength plays a huge factor in our shows. This is why I turn to yoga and Pilates for this exact reason. Activating muscles while holding postures improves my breathing and builds overall strength. Finding your breath on stage during a fast tarantella is crucial to surviving our tour. Partnering with lifts requires brute strength from both dancers.

Once toned, stretched, rehearsed and sculpted, it is time to take it to the stage or arena. Nothing prepares the mind for a performance like getting into a costume. This is where a dancer becomes the character and starts to feel excited. This one might be obvious, but a costume can enhance or take away from a beautiful dance, or any performance. Making sure that the costume matches the feeling the dance is conveying. Being precise about the time period is also a concern of mine. Sometimes in a one hour show we don't have enough time to change the entire costume so we may stick to just one time period or just one region of Italy. I offer a brief note to the audience to help explain the dance, the region and time period.

Costume colors might spark a certain tone or vibe for a dance. Having a costume fitting with the dancers before we perform is a must. I can only imagine the importance for the gladiator's armor to fit. I cringe when I see dancers on stage tugging on leotards or pulling at straps. The costumes fitting properly on the dancers will not only look great, but also give confidence to the dancer. Straps that fall or pants that are too big are a disaster waiting to happen. It becomes all that the audience notices instead of the movement I worked so hard on to achieve. Doing a test at rehearsals with a few different looks helps to see which one looks best. I never wait until the last minute to just throw something together. This is a recipe for failure and never works out.

One of my male dancers wore ill-fitting pants to a performance for an outdoor festival. This was one of the first few years I took the company on tour. He had the most gorgeous jumps and leaps out of the group, so of course I put him center stage to show off these courageous moves. Then, after the most graceful jump, I heard a sound.

Rip!

Oh No! This can't be happening.

Not too many things get my attention during a show, but the sound of fabric tearing is at or near the top of the list. My company was still young, and I was doing my best to make great first impressions so we were invited back. When I heard the rip, I was in the midst of a turning sequence near him. As the director, I am already trying to think of ways to help the situation. My brain splits in half, part dancer, part director. Thankfully, we only had a few more moves of that dance before I could get him off stage and assess the situation. The group takes their bow, and we exit off stage. I motion for our MC to vamp. I rushed over to my dancer to see how bad the situation was. I go behind the stage shielded from the audience and ask what had happened. My dancer explains that he ripped his pants from the zipper to the back along the seam. Thank goodness for black underwear underneath his black pants. He was known for wearing colorful boxer shorts, but thankfully he listened and wore his black underwear. I looked around and knew we didn't have an extra pair of pants and neither did he. So, I found my black duct tape. Yes, thanks to my father, I carried duct tape in my dance bag and still do for any emergencies. One never knows when you might have to become MacGyver. At the speed of light, dancers help him affix the tape to cover up the gaping hole to get through the rest of the show. No more jumps for the next two dances, fortunately.

Lesson learned, try on costumes before a performance and practice all the moves full out to test what works and what might rip. I also bring a spare shirt and pants now to every performance. Let's just say he let it rip that day for the show. Not sure if the audience noticed the rip in his pants, but his outstanding showcase of jumps impressed everyone including me.

Sometimes the costume itself can spark an idea to create a new dance piece. Thrift shopping for costumes is exciting. It's the hunt for a great treasure you might find. It's an easy way to find unique items at a low cost. Once I walk into a thrift store, I see a whole slew of stories just hanging there waiting for me to bring them to life. I can visualize characters and different moods to explore as I sweep each hanger of clothing in the store. Some captivating dresses and accessories were found at various stores over the years. Once purchased, washed, and adorned with some ribbons or fresh buttons the look is stupendo!

Creating characters from a handful of accessories I gathered can be exciting on stage. If you can afford to hire a seamstress, do it. They are worth gold. I have had a few costumes created from a sketch and it's always worth the time to get what you really want for your dance. Invest in a few pieces that can stand the test of time and weather the many miles on tour. Try to reuse them in different ways by adding a new trim or another layer to a skirt. This has always worked for my company so that we can continue to use them and save some cash along the way. It can be expensive to buy new costumes each year. Finding new ways to save or reuse costumes from the past can help sustain the company. A button-down shirt might become a short skirt or cut up to make an apron for a different region of Italy. Using lighter fabrics to brave the heat on our summer tours along with adding rubber non-skid pads to the bottom of our shoes to keep us from falling. These are all innovative ways I have adapted costumes for the company. I bet our gladiator friends would have benefited from some lighter weight fabrics and rubber shoe soles! Occasionally, we go barefoot on better flooring and indoor stages.

Seeing the Colosseum flooded my mind with multiple ideas for choreography, costumes and stories to share with the American audiences. I felt the intensity when we emerged in the stands and saw the full scope of the entire stadium. Just to be inside this infamous structure that millions of people see often was captivating. This wasn't my first time inside the Colosseum, but every time I experience it, I see the history and grandeur. There is always something new to observe and learn.

When we left the stadium, outside there were men dressed up as senators, gladiators and centurions, ready to snap some pictures with you for a few euros. We had some fun and got some candid shots with the performers for a few minutes as the sun started to burn away the gray clouds. We noticed what we thought was funny, and certainly only an Italian sight. Some police officers were in a discussion with some of the performers dressed as Roman Legionnaires. It was comical to see the old Roman uniformed men, juxtaposed against current law enforcement, both seemly very serious in conversation, compared to the tourists laughing it up with the other performers in the Piazza.

Our history lesson of the Roman Empire continued with more ruins near the Colosseum. The sun was now shining brightly in the sky and the temperature was starting to climb. We walked through the ruins of the Roman Forum, the remnants of the governmental buildings from the Empire. Valerio showed us Caesar Augustus' house as well as next door, Augustus' wife, Livi's house. This was also part of the archaeological site.

We jokingly remarked to Valerio that it made sense they fell in love since they were already neighbors, and it seemed like a small-town love story. He was immediately perplexed. He thought he had explained the history incorrectly and was very quick to try to correct our thinking. It was important to him that we did not come away with a misunderstanding of history. It was fun to twist some revisionist history around on him, but at the same time I really respected his commitment to making sure we had a better grasp of Roman history. I doubt I would be as invested in explaining Thomas Jefferson's relationship with his wife to foreign visitors. He wrote the Declaration of Independence, lived in Monticello and was president number three. Any other facts I could remember to tell my friend would be a bonus.

Valerio explained Julius Caesar's rise to power, and that Augustus was Julius Caesar's cousin. He reminded me of Shakespeare's famous play depicting how Augustus became emperor and that his reign was characterized by the Pax Romana. The third fact was one I remembered from Western Civilization in college, but I probably haven't thought about it since. Valerio was kind enough to explain so many of the nuisances I had forgotten. We continued chatting, laughing and walking through the ruins and gardens.

By now the sun was hot, and Valerio was still wearing his jacket. He said that Italians don't take their jackets off until summer. Either way, it was time to get out of the sun and get a refreshing drink. More and more tourists had come out for the nice weather and our tour was complete. Time to treat our gracious tour guide to lunch and tell him our stories about visiting the Vatican the day before.

We had tickets for Vatican City. Immediately arriving in Rome, with no rest, running on excitement and a cappuccino, we went to the Vatican to tour the museums, visit St Peter's Basilica and the Sistine Chapel. I remember getting to the entrance vividly, high walls, the imposing Swiss Guard dressed in their colorful uniforms and a very impressive doorway. I took my first of thousands of pictures on our first day there. I was eager to show Greg all of these captivating historical landmarks.

After entering the country within a county, we wandered through a museum appreciating the large sculptures and artifacts and eventually met up with a tour that was going into the Vatican Grottoes. These were tombs where previous popes occupied their final resting places. It was enthralling. The dates of the tombs reach so far back into the past, it is hard to comprehend. My mind just spins at this point. It is interesting how in Europe, seeing a date of sometime in the 1660's isn't considered old. That was more than a century before the United States adopted the Constitution! One of the churches we visited in Bologna dated back to the 700's.

Walking through the tombs and sarcophagus, we noticed a group of people praying and crying at one of the alcoves. We slowed down our pace and became quiet. I could feel the hairs on my skin stand at attention. When we got closer, we saw that it was the tomb of Pope John Paul II. My eyes began to water and the lump in my throat was growing. This visit was in 2010, and pilgrims were still coming to his tomb and holding vigil over five years after his death. Until that point, in our jet lagged state and casual outfits, we hadn't grasped the significance of the tour we were on. Each sarcophagus or tomb contained a human person who was not only a former pope or royalty, but someone who had touched others' lives or had inspired others to follow a cause bigger than themselves. This moment stopped both of us in our tracks.

I reflected upon taking my company to Italy when we danced a tarantella for Pope John Paul II not far from his tomb. All those memories flashed before me in my mind. Even though time is a constant, it is moments like this that make it feel like life is a roller coaster going so fast you can't catch your breath.

The Sistine Chapel is always mesmerizing and outstanding to view. Michelangelo's 'Creation of Adam' is one of the pieces that required me to stop and stare for a great amount of time. Greg and I had sore necks from looking up so much after going through the chapel. There is so much to admire.

Our adventure in the capital of Italy was a small taste of the Lazio region where the seven hills of Rome meet the Appian Way. We threw our three coins in the Trevi Fountain and walked up the Spanish Steps. We ate delicious pizza outside the Pantheon and refreshed our water bottles at the beautiful fountain in Piazza Navona. There is so much history to see, to experience, to taste and to admire in Rome. As the saying goes, *veni, vidi, vici*. I came, I saw, I conquered. Time spent in the eternal city encourages me to stand strong, be brave, and lead with the heart.

My husband and I head for the airport in Rome to take our flight back to the United States. Our ten wonderful days in Italy went by so fast. We arrived at the gate for our flight back, but it was super crowded and there was nowhere to sit. So, we decided to walk around for a few minutes. We are now far from our gate. I stopped into a gift shop to grab a magazine to read. I look around and he is nowhere to be found. I panicked for just a few minutes and then I spotted him. He was distracted by a *panini* stand and ventured over there to get a sandwich. Greg is not of Italian descent, but I swear his stomach is. I tell him not to take too long because we will be boarding soon, and we have a bit of a walk to get back to our gate.

A few minutes go by, and I see my husband carrying on a conversation with the man who is making his sandwich. Greg has picked up a few Italian words and phrases over the years that have helped him through our travels. He was proudly using them to order his sandwich. He is gesturing to the man with confidence saying, "*Questo panino per favore!*" this sandwich please. I rolled my eyes thinking, *why is he getting a sandwich now when we are on a time limit.* Greg just couldn't resist one last taste of Italy and wanted to savor it on the plane. I didn't want to leave Italy either, but I also didn't want to miss our ride home.

The man asked if Greg wanted his sandwich toasted.

"Certo!" Greg said with a large smile. Of course, he does. Toasting his sandwich is not helping us with our tight timeline. Our plane is going to leave soon. I was starting to pace back and forth dragging my suitcase along to try to calm down.

My brain began scrambling with what if questions like: *What if we miss our flight? What if there isn't another flight today?* Then the other side of my brain said, *who cares, you are in Italy!*

As Greg's sandwich goes into the toaster, I hear on the overhead speaker in the airport:

Signore e Signora Harsh, please report to your gate.

OH NO! I think that's us!

I tapped Greg on the shoulder and frantically whispered, *"Did you hear that? That's us, Greg. We must go! PRONTO!"*

Greg doesn't believe that was our name being called. He was intent on watching his glorious sandwich getting a golden tan. But then I hear it again over the speaker:

Signore e Signora Harsh please report to your gate for your flight.

Greg's eyes grew twice in size and now understands that we must go. I motioned to the kind man making his sandwich and said *Andiamo!* He nodded and wrapped the sandwich quickly. Greg paid and grabbed the *panino.*

"Grazie!" we shouted, as we ran to the gate to catch our flight.

We were pretty far from our gate, so it was time to hustle. As if we were running in a track meet, we are at full speed rolling our bags to our gate. Greg reminds me these are the times we train for when we work out. All those early morning workouts were paying off, at least we hoped. We finally made it to our gate number out of breath. The sitting area was completely empty. I looked at the ticket booth and the lady had concern in her eyes but smiled politely to try to cover it up. We gave her our tickets and exhaled.

Signore e Signora Harsh? She asks.

In unison we said, *SI!*

As we started boarding, I noticed the stares from the people already seated. I wondered how long they were all waiting on us.

I thought we were the last people getting on. Then, I see one man behind us entering. Greg nudged me as if to say, see, we weren't the last ones on the plane. I gave him a look as if to say, not now.

Mostly filled with Americans, I could see judgment making a debut appearance. Embarrassment permeated my skin, so I kept my eyes forward. Greg was so content and had completely embraced the Italian lifestyle with his big grin on his face admiring his *panino*. I was thrilled he enjoyed another adventure. However, I was trying to calm my nerves from the intense marathon we had just completed. I felt as if there should have been some kind of medal ceremony with our accomplishment of making it back to the plane in record time. I would have settled for a door prize.

We had stowed our bags, got settled and strapped into our seat belts for takeoff. I began my usual ritual of prayers and gratitude for another voyage of seeing friends and family along with the fantastic things I had learned. Once in the air, I began a prayer for a safe flight home and was distracted when I heard paper rattling. It's my husband, Greg, unwrapping his sandwich. He just couldn't wait to unveil this masterpiece as if it was crafted by Michelangelo himself. Seriously, I think choirs sang when he opened it. It was ***that*** spectacular. All eyes including myself looked over at him to investigate what he was doing. I can't explain the enticing aroma that dominated the space from his *panino.* The smell infused the air so much, the flight attendant had a look of jealousy. It was a delicious blend of roasted peppers, melted provolone cheese and various cured Italian meats between two toasted freshly baked pieces of bread. I guarantee nothing like that was going to be served on our flight home. He was smart enough to buy it.

Greg realized at this point, I was not mad at him and would appreciate a bite or two. While he wasn't willing to share with everyone, he was willing to share with me. My mouth was watering. He knew that even though it wasn't the best time to order food, it was well worth the trouble. He reaches over and offers half of his sandwich to share. After just a few bites, I knew that this work of art was worth the wait. As other passengers found new distractions, like the inflight entertainment, Greg and I began a conversation of our spectacular voyage and all the new layers of Italian culture we discovered. He is a great travel partner and always listens to his instincts when we travel. He makes my pursuit to preserve my heritage a carousel of love.

La Vinca or Bal de truc

While the origin of this dance is unknown, it is often found in several northern regions of Italy. I am told this dance is taught to young children, but I have also seen adults enjoy this dance as well. The movements and attitude of this dance makes me think of Rome because of the name La Vinca (the win). It's a dance of a dueling conversation between the men and women as they express themselves with intensity.

The 2/4 tempo which alternates from a skipping figure with stomping, clapping and finger wagging. The dance resembles several other folk dances from central and eastern Europe.

The dance begins in a circle by skipping with your partner side by side. The man on the inside and the woman on the outside. His hand is on her right shoulder, and she is holding on to his hands. One variation I came across, dancers take sixteen steps clockwise and then sixteen steps counterclockwise instead of skipping.

After the skipping ends, face your partner. The gentleman stomps his feet, right, left, right then the woman claps three times. This is her answering his stomps. It seems like a challenge at this point.

Staying face to face both men and women shake their right index finger three times, then the left index finger three times at their partner near each other's faces. You will hear the timing in the music for the exact rhythm. After this section, each dancer takes a small turn individually to the right. This stomping, clapping and shaking repeats once more then back to the skipping from the beginning.

While skipping with their partners there is a moment where the entire group holds hands in a larger circle and accents the rhythm with a singular stomp on count 1. The dancers break from the big circle and go back to holding their partner seamlessly, across the back of their shoulder. The men pull out a handkerchief and wave it straight up with their left hand on beat one. It's a nice transitional moment with a spark using the handkerchief. It checks off many of the choreography elements like using level and directional changes. By adding the stomps, it gives accents to the movement which make it interesting to participate and observe. The women wave their skirts back and forth while they are skipping, which adds a bit of whimsy and flirtation.

The dance continues with another round of the stomps, claps and finger waving. Some versions have the couples separate and skip with all men in one circle and all women in another circle. Then the couples can re-emerge together in two lines facing the audience at the end with women in front and men behind as the women bow and the men wave their handkerchief to the sky.

Who wins this challenge? That is up to you! Filled with a winning spirit, in the next chapter you will get a backstage view of how I put my dance shows together.

5,6,7,8

- What gladiator qualities do you possess?
- How do you prepare for your personal arena?
- What armor do you put on in life?
- Do you know your own city's history?

Inspired by a busker in Italy, I created a tango solo.

Choreography tools and Performance tips

Studying the formations of northern folk dances gave me insight to the different regions of Italy as well as the choreographer's mind from hundreds of years ago. Stepping inside the formations of diamond shapes or strong lines that change and intersect when dancers change partners, spoke volumes to me. Their organizational skills were outstanding as well as aesthetically pleasing to watch. Then again, this shouldn't surprise me when I look at architecture and fashion. The dance formations demonstrated northern Italians were very direct, precise and kept an orderly life. Directional changes can create texture for choreography like textured fabric on a great jacket or gown. To me, this was like reading that choreographer's diary. They are showing me their inspirations, motivations and goals. A little piece of them lives on by me recreating and sharing dances.

When I arrange these dances, I plot out how dancers enter and exit the piece first, which leads to better organization. Making use of diagonals brings depth to a piece. The longest straight line on stage is the diagonal stretching from back corner to front corner. Finding ways in the middle of a phrase of movement to change direction can bring a spark of surprise and dynamic. I try placing leaps going on a diagonal or straight towards the audience instead of straight across the stage. Making dancers turn and switch lines brings excitement to the piece. I never let dancers linger in straight lines too long. More than a couple phrases of movement will seem stagnant. Being specific with directions will keep routines clean and create interest at the same time.

When creating a contemporary piece, another tool I use is level change. Seeking out moments in my choreography where I could change a level by adding a jump to add height or flowing arm movements downward. Finding a variety of levels allows the eye to find the highs and lows of your dance, mimicking real life. Presenting high, medium and low levels offers a nice variety.

Depending on the dance surface, I also create some floor work to indulge in low level work. Specifically for a contemporary piece, I create a phrase of movement on the floor. Dropping to move onto or near the floor, allows for those moments of low. I reserve time while choreographing a piece to explore lower levels. I watch my dance from beginning to end with a checklist to see if I have high points and low points in the dance, to generate enough contrast. A dancer might be on one knee or lunging, reaching toward the ground. Some of the folk dances, like in a Sicilian tarantella, have a section or two where the man kneels, and the woman hops around him. This is a great example where both high and low levels come together to create an interesting picture.

La furlana has levels built into the dance by doing a waltz step, finding the highs and lows by bending the knees and going up onto the ball of the feet. Seeing the crown move up and down exploring the space as if the couple was moving about the kingdom. This calm and serene movement is quite the contrast to the southern dances. Many of the southern folk dances have an earthy grounded quality utilizing a low level by keeping the knees bent throughout the dance. Then, a vibrant arm will soar into the air like a bird when they twirl about faster and faster. This unexpectedness in the dance makes it exhilarating and wild.

To achieve a better comprehension of the levels in dance, I play a game with my students called sit, stand, or kneel. Learning this game in college, students change from pose to pose when the instructor says the word "change." Changing from sitting to standing, standing to kneeling, or kneeling to sitting and so on helps the dancers explore levels and find new pathways to get from one level to the other. This exploration can open the imagination to produce something unique. There are a variety of ways to explore the same pose, two examples of kneeling are a child's pose in yoga or a man proposing. Adding the transitions to these poses can completely change the flow or story to a piece. Dancers can tend to fall into patterns and watching how others approach the game helps dancers break their own habits and to stretch their repertoire.

Varying the tempo with your body will spice up a dance. Various folk dances like *Giga Emiliana* change the speed of the footwork midway within the dance. We go from sliding our feet on the down beat of the music to performing a syncopated rhythm, like a polka step, with our partner. Varying the tempo of the movements can evolve the choreography to seem more sophisticated.

Even when a song remains at the same tempo, there are still ways for the dancer to adjust. I listen to the song I want to use several times. I find a horn section or piano part to follow and create a phrase of movement by imitating the melody with my feet or arms. Taking this idea one step further, I could have my feet go with the downbeat while my arms follow the melody in the song. Figuring out where to place the slower and faster sections can be confusing at first, but with more practice, these choreographic ideas become easier. I started using this strategy with solos more often than with group numbers. Switching the tempo of moves too often offers a playground of chaos. Keeping it simple and using it sparingly is best.

From the folk dances I have studied, a slight tempo change is built in. If live musicians are playing, then you could be at the mercy of them varying the tempo. Southern tarantellas embody an increasing tempo to pump up the heart rate and sweat out the poison from the spider bite. Tempo changes enliven folk dances empowering a community spirit. One moment your body is swaying from side to side waiting your turn to go into the center of the circle, and the next minute you and your partner's feet are on fire from footwork that encapsulates the melody of a mandolin.

The exploration of patterns on stage can revitalize any dance and illustrate dynamics. Finding couples in straight lines creating a clear and precise path makes it easy to see which couple is out of line or not in sync with others. Being in straight lines, from an entertainment point of view, could come across as boring to watch unless the other choreography tools I mentioned are applied.

Allegro Dance Company performs authentic Italian dances to preserve but we also perform and create dances that are inspired by and reflect the culture. I am always on a quest for ways to tell present day stories about Italian lifestyle. My piece called *Metro Dance* is a great example of when choreographic tools met inspiration.

Greg and I rode trains and metros daily. It was the easiest and fastest way to go from one city to another. Paying close attention to the entire system of transportation, I noticed it had a rhythm. My dancer brain took over. Movement appears to me everywhere, which causes me to see choreography in my mind. The rhythm of each train coming in and out along with the sounds when it's in motion, gave me an idea. On a whim, I pulled out my phone on one of our rides on the metro and recorded the sounds of stops along with the whistles and bells of each stop. This also included the sound of the doors opening and closing. I don't know why I found this so intriguing, but I did that day and kept that logged into my phone for a while.

Sometimes ideas have to simmer in my brain before they are fully cooked. Then when I got home, it hit me. The idea for choreography came so fast it was like I was watching a movie in my head. I had been examining and memorizing metro and train maps in Italy for some time. I would count how many stops to each city to properly plan out our adventures. Noticing that each train path was colored coordinated with primary colors like red, yellow, green and purple.

That's it!

The inspiration was now clear. The Milan metro map was interesting to me because when looking at it from above, it revealed specific patterns. These patterns became floor patterns for sketching out a dance. Deciding how dancers take a path on stage can greatly influence where other dancers come and go. I once had a choreographer tell me that when they choreograph a large group number, they work out the entrances and exits first, then start to fill in with the meat of the choreography. I use this strategy when working on musicals often because I need to know where the characters are coming from and where they need to be before the next scene.

The more I looked at the metro map, the more compelled I became to choreograph a contemporary piece about travel in Italy. The pathways were all laid out for me with this map. I started to put my thoughts together about what I wanted the audience to feel or understand during the piece. As I raced to catch many metros in Italy, I wanted to include that feeling in the dance. I positioned each dancer at the beginning of one of the metro routes. The dancer had the map to know the path they would take on the stage. Green, for example, went in a straight line then turned slightly right then straight and finally made a 90-degree angle right. I went through each color and route with the dancers.

Next, I went over timing, so there were no collisions. Like the trains at a station, timing is everything. Seeing the dancers work closely and figure out who was going in front and how to avoid a collision was gratifying. Teamwork speaks volumes when you see this collaboration in rehearsal.

Deciding how they would travel on those paths, I took my cue from the map. Some trains were faster than others and got to their destination sooner. So, I did the same. There were traveling phrases filled with quick, small jumps and fast turns. Other phrases were slower with a simple walking combination and flowing arms. When the dancers came to their final destination, they froze in a pose as if they were waiting for a train to arrive. I was the last dancer to arrive at my destination, but I rushed to get to my spot to give a feeling of making it just in time. Real life is often seen in art. I'm not usually late for events nor transportation, but punctuality can be tough.

We took a beat for breath at that moment collectively before the next phrase of movement began.

This modern jazz number went on to incorporate angular arm movements that played with space and time alongside the winding pathways I drew out for the dancers. A few moments of being in sync were found from time to time in the choreography. These sections of moving as a group were mixed with break out solo phrases. Various phrases were repeated from the beginning of the choreography to bring the storyline full circle. Repeating this section acted as a flashback in the story of catching the metro.

Solo moments made the piece pop with a fresh take on transportation and an opportunity to place a few extraordinary moves which highlighted special skills of certain dancers. At one point, we used the word metro as inspiration for movement. We spelled out the word metro with our bodies in different ways. Some dancers traced the letters out by using their arm or leg, others shaped their bodies in the form of each letter and used a transitional move like a turn or walking to get to the next letter. This became my favorite section of the dance because the principles of choreography were all used at once without it being too overwhelming to watch.

For costuming, I assigned specific dancers the color of the train route they were portraying. We wore colored t-shirts and black leggings with sneakers. The variety of colors on stage gave a cheerful and vibrant quality, especially to see it juxtaposed against a dark stage. To enhance the fast pace, I layered a fun upbeat song with the metro sounds I recorded on my phone to offer a realistic atmosphere of the station. This dance was well received and audiences of all ages responded better than I expected.

This wouldn't be the first time I was compelled to choreograph based on patterns. Influenced by textures in Italian fashion as well as architecture, I often sketch what I see and evolve these designs into a floor pattern for choreography. Referring to photographs of my travels, I look at the details of buildings like a repeated motif I saw on the top of Doge's Palace in Venice. This Gothic architecture had two lines coming to a strong point. I took this same idea to create pathways with dancers beginning in two lines and then coming to a center point on the stage.

Other inspirations might come from textures I see in fabrics, like the beautiful brocade fabrics I found in Florence with soft edges with shapes and delicate flowers. Occasionally, I look at pasta shapes and contemplate how I could create these same shapes with the body. I know this sounds a bit off the wall, but it's where my artistic brain goes when I see something that strikes me. All of these ideas swirl in my head until I draw them out. From the sketch, it becomes a road map of sorts for my dancers to follow like the metro map.

This big world we live in is breath-taking and exhilarating if you just stop long enough to notice and absorb it. That's the key, noticing the smallest details around you. Being inspired like this is my go-to exercise to get out of a rut in choreography. I think it can help anyone get back on track in life.

When I see something that has a beautiful pattern, I take a blank piece of paper and draw what spoke to me. It could be the shape of a flower petal or the constellation that night. Anything is fair game. I drew a spider for one of my Sicilian tarantellas where the dancers formed a circle to make the body of the spider and then danced in and out of the circle forming small lines to make eight legs. If viewed from above the spider would appear to be crawling. It was a cool effect and wowed the audience for sure. This unique approach offered an innovative yet clear path of where the dancers should begin on stage.

Organizing this way assists me greatly in plotting out formation changes which can make a big impact. These methods might be a little out of the box, but it makes it memorable for both the dancers and the audience. I always receive positive feedback when I use this as my process to choreograph a modern or jazz piece. When choreography comes from a place of truth and inspiration, it resonates with the audience.

Being still in a dance might sound strange, but this is also an important element. I revere choreography that rests for a beat or two. It's bold and brave at the same time. It allows the audience to absorb the moment. Stillness can be inserted after performing a lively phrase to create contrast in a piece or to mark a moment of importance. As I work through my choreography, I check where stillness could be placed. I have created solos that started with stillness and then escalated to tell a story of bleakness or loneliness. The opposite is just as interesting. Stillness can also be a powerful ending as a dance coming to a complete stop.

Finding serenity where the body settles or a group abruptly stops to notice something on stage can pack a punch. Oftentimes, stillness makes a bigger statement than an impressive quantity of *pirouettes* or athletic feats. History harbors a litany of dances that beautifully utilizes stillness as a special moment. Dancers in tableaux hold poses for great periods of time in various ballets. As every musician sees a rest on their sheet of music, a dancer pauses for tranquility or quietude. Holding for a breath or two could be just what the piece needs to improve.

Folk dances in general usually repeat a section of the dance so that everyone can participate. When teaching folk dance to students or new dancers in my company, they are grateful for this element, so they have more opportunities to catch on to the sequence of moves. I, too, use this idea in my own choreography for various styles of dance. For example, let's say six counts of eight is the length of my dance phrase. I can repeat this same phrase in the dance later at some point to give the audience familiarity by building a motif.

This same idea goes for repeating a move in groups of three, like three quick jumps or three turns in a row that travel. Sometimes an interesting arm phrase or partner hold needs to be seen again to absorb. I make sure not to go overboard with repeating a move since it can become monotonous. This repetition of movement can create a feeling of comfort and ease. Repeating a move three times makes it memorable and appealing. You don't have to repeat a phrase or move exactly like you did earlier. You can offer variations or perform it in retrograde.

Many of the Italian folk dances have a clear story with a beginning, middle, and end. I find myself writing down their main ideas as bullet points to make sure I have the dance correctly. Each folk dance has a story to be told with clarity. Remembering the purpose of dance is to communicate a thought, idea or emotion. If I am creating a modern piece, I do the same by listing bullet points so that my message is clear.

In the 15th and 16th centuries, intricate set designs were created to enhance their storytelling. While this isn't possible with my dance company traveling to outdoor festivals, we do bring large props from time to time to embellish the scene. Even though the performances in the past were done by candlelight, I am sure they thought about how the glow of the candles affected the portrayal of the performers.

The use of lighting can be beneficial to bring the story or mood across the finish line. No matter if it is a moody jazz number or a folk dance portraying goddesses, lighting is something I have to consider if we are performing in a theater. What about the lighting for Catherine the Great's wedding? It must have been magical and romantic.

Pondering over whether I need a spotlight or shin busters to create a 3D effect of the dancers' bodies or choosing the color of lighting can enhance the costuming. A talented lighting designer assists by setting a mood with great effects that magnify your movement. For me, lighting is the jewelry to a dance piece adding sparkle and refinement. Thinking about lighting design first can set my imagination in motion. Choosing colors and brightness can change the appearance of the costumes. If you are dancing outdoors, like we do for most festivals, a ray of sunshine bounces beams off of gems on a headpiece while a few clouds can cast interesting shadows on our faces.

Once a piece of choreography is finished, I step out of a dance to walk around the entire rehearsal space to view the dance from the back, the sides, and the front. Watching the dance from all sides of the space brings insight that is imperative before we perform. New angles of the dance that the audience should enjoy can be found. Adjusting the dancers to achieve this new 360-degree perspective allows me to refresh the spacing or bring attention to the technique that might be in need of improvement.

When we are getting closer to performing the choreography, the first thing I tell myself and my dancers is to breathe. Yes, breathing sounds so easy, however, we can become extremely nervous on stage and forget to breathe. By taking a few deep breaths backstage before the show can calm the nerves and clear the mind. It improves our concentration and reminds the body to breathe through each move on stage. Exhaling on the large movements like kicks or leaps will increase their height and make it look effortless. Breathing helps the muscles perform more efficiently and lessens the chances of injuries.

Personally, I close my eyes and visualize the entire piece move by move in my mind's eye. This helps my body and mind recall the movement and boosts confidence on stage. If short on time, I visualize the first few moves to feel ready. This method stops the body from freezing up on stage and forgetting what you are about to do. Visualization is a powerful exercise for any dancer. Picturing the audience applauding for a performance promotes positivity.

It never hurts to manifest an awesome show.

Inhale applause, exhale greatness.

On the day of a show, fruit and eggs are my go-to breakfast with a refreshing hot green tea. Depending on what time the show is, a small serving of pasta makes a debut with green vegetables and lemon water. As my muscles and bones remind me of the many years of experience, I have learned to take great care of my body and fuel it up properly so that I am fully prepared. My dance bag is complete with a water bottle, granola snacks or a banana as well as a few mints for breath. Keeping fit and staying well is a daily ritual and routine for dancers. Being comfortable while traveling is a must. My warm-up outfit must be just as soft and comfortable as my favorite pillow and blanket that is also packed.

Silence or music, which do you need to get into the zone? I need pure silence to prepare. Locating a space for a few deep breaths in and out generates calmness and clarity. This grounds me enough to stay present before I walk onto a stage. Some of my dancers like a few minutes of silence to quiet their mind and others will listen to their favorite song right before they go on to get them hyped up. I tell them to find something that works for them. Whatever it takes to get in the mood and bring their fullest potential out. Stirring up a positive attitude before you go on stage is key to a great performance. If a dancer is not in the mood, it reads on stage and the audience knows it. That bad energy travels faster than the speed of light it seems and reaches everyone around. So, keeping it light and positive is best.

Arriving at a venue backstage there are a few rituals I like to initiate. Connecting as a group to feel cohesive comes as a high priority. After we set up our things and get warmed up and stretched, we take our places backstage. Giving high fives or winks with a genuine smile can let everyone know you are in this together. When dancing with a partner, we tend to offer them a hug before we embark on a dance. Teamwork really does make the dream work, at least with my company.

Gathering in a small circle our hands reach out to connect. Speaking softly about how grateful we are to be together the feeling of community begins. Being apart for so long during the pandemic has reinforced how much we need each other in this moment of holding hands again.

Connected as a group, we glance at everyone in the circle to vibe as one on stage.

Northern dances of Italy demand proper posture, precision and utmost attention. That can be a tall order if you are not prepared. Being the full package on stage can be lost if a dancer doesn't connect with the other dancers or the audience. To perform on stage with your mind, body, and spirit showcases the beauty and power of movement. A great deal of partner work requires concentration in the northern dances as shown in *Circolo Circasso*. It becomes crucial to remain mentally present and aligned with your partner. Being physically attached with hands or arms and not having a weak grip as in *Saltarello Bolognese* avoids mishaps and falls. Engaging with a partner in their eyes is enchanting. Northern dances pull back the curtain where the story of adoration, power, or becoming a creature from the beyond is seen with just a look.

Once our feet hit the stage, it is time to draw the audience in. Captivating them to witness our stories, feel the emotions and win their applause brings purpose to the performance.

How does this audience connection happen?

We must relate to the audience by becoming the characters on stage through movement. Energy, eye contact and being truthful with our performance forms a union. I have witnessed performances where the dancer's only goal was to show off with no intention of offering a story or emotion. Our goal is to include the audience and start a relationship in each show in various ways. For example, opening up our circle formations in a tarantella to a half circle allows the audience to feel as though they complete our circle. In a northern dance, we might rotate a straight line to face the audience for an up-close view of the intricate footwork. Audiences shouldn't struggle to see or understand what's going on. By making these few adjustments, we bond with our crowd, and they see us in a new light.

Dancers perform with their entire body and their faces define the emotions. Over the years, I have seen some weird facial expressions during shows like squinting eyes or half smiles that are misunderstood. Each folk dance has a story to tell and a character to portray which should be reflected on our faces as well as the motions. Every dancer must understand the story to properly express it from head to toe.

Researching the time period and the people of a certain region, their motivations could be different. A regal noble with raised eyebrows and pursed lips has a look of pride. Yet joy expressed with a wide smile presents a healing release like in a southern tarantella. Each dance holds a vast array of expressions we could embody. Reserved northern dances require a polite smile with a straight posture like in *Saltarello Bolognese*. Southern dances are filled with intense facials like deep eye contact and wide smiles. Their upper body has a more relaxed posture and is seen especially in the tarantella from Calabria. Rehearsing different facial expressions by looking in a mirror improves the performer. Watching a rehearsal on video and practicing in the mirror brings a continuous evolution of the dancer's range and abilities.

Self-esteem can instantly diminish when reviewing a video or seeing the reflection in a mirror. A dancer can pinpoint where their abilities can improve, but the list might never end. It can take a toll on our mental health. Not only is recording dances for preservation and recall a must, but it forces us to prepare and improve. Seeing both weakness and strengths balance us. Remembering these are mere ways to improve technique and performance quality. It is best to know sooner rather than later how it appears.

Swept up in the spotlights, intoxicating music and majestic costumes, gratitude is stepped on like a welcome mat. Egos can expand like an accordion on tour and opportunities can be easily taken for granted. Seeing the older generations in the crowd reminds me to be thankful and that time is fleeting. Not everyone receives these opportunities in their lifetime to perform nor share their talents in this capacity. Remember, we are here to preserve a heritage as well as entertain.

Thanking backstage help is also part of my gratitude practice. Changing costumes in under a minute is a feat and having those extra hands to help is crucial. Switching costumes to represent different regions of Italy brings excitement as well as education to our performance. This might require pulling on a different skirt, swapping out a vest or pinning on a new headpiece. Having someone there to hold your costume to change or assist you with zipping up or unbuttoning is needed to make the show run smoothly.

Depending on which region in the north, the costumes can require different headpieces or accessories. They have a soft palate of colors with hues of yellow and green or blue, while southern regions are saturated with darker shades of red, black and other jewel tones. Each dancer has a partner to help them in the group to make this costume magic happen effortlessly. This presto change has an order and is rehearsed. Showing appreciation for that partner after the show builds respect. Gratitude improves our well-being and helps us be our best on and off stage. We must keep evolving as we gain more experience.

Maintaining a great mindset prepares a dancer for life off stage. I resist engaging in negative chatter with others backstage. Words do matter so why not put only positive vibes out there in the universe. Besides, no artist wants to hear about bad news before they are about to perform. I encourage everyone backstage to stay positive, breathe and be mindful of the conversations they have before taking the stage. That positivity can make or break a performance. I want my partner to be calm and in a good mood especially if I am going to be lifted by him. Having upbeat conversations builds trust and happiness. I frequently hear dancers speak about a lack of energy backstage. Saying this aloud doesn't serve any purpose. It only brings you as well as others down.

Instead, I say, "We are going to have a great show!" Boosting everyone's energy and attitude helps bring some zest back to the mind. The body will believe what you tell it. So always say positive things!

After finding a few breaths before the show begins, I prompt the dancers to end all conversations as we walk onto the stage.

Inhale and exhale.

Touring isn't for everyone. Driving to different destinations can be exhausting and can take a toll on the body when you are obligated to sit for hours while driving to the next venue. Cross-training with resistance bands and yoga can ease muscles with those long drives. Resting at a park to stretch and eat along the journey helps tremendously with our well-being. This is my advice for traveling in Italy as well. There are various places to stop and rest before heading on to another city. It's important to take care of yourself so that your eternal flame doesn't get extinguished.

Bouncing from city to city, we never come across the same set up or stage. Stages can vary greatly with different venues. I remind the venues we need a specific square footage of space. Sometimes that goes on deaf ears. If we are offered a professional dance floor with lights, we count our blessings. These variations of stages can cause problems for our showcase. Going from rehearsing in a studio or smaller space to a bigger stage can be quite challenging. The opposite is also true by showing up to perform in a space that is too small. When we perform, dancers need to take up as much space as possible. We call it dancing full out! Spend every last ounce of energy and extend all the limbs to their fullest potential. One must take up a great amount of space to perform in stadiums and larger festivals. This allows the audience to see the details of the work. It is like taking a magnifying glass to our show. Northern dances require us to be close in tight lines like soldiers, while the southern tarantellas are a bit freer flowing and wild with organic formations that beg for more room to roam. I remind dancers to stop marking in the rehearsals and go full out so we can be consistent with our spacing. This trains the body to be consistent. I can't imagine any nobility doing a movement halfway that lacked energy or fervor. It would be frowned upon greatly.

Like a filing system, my mind has to remember a tremendous number of details while on tour. Recalling all the announcements, what to pack, the show choreography, and the costume changes can be all consuming at first. But with three decades under my belt, my lists have become more detailed and categorized. Our one-hour showcase has transitions between dances to memorize, props and costume changes along with the order of the show. Each detail down to the music transitions must be well thought out and timed.

I create a guide sheet backstage that helps us all stay on task. This guide contains the order of the show, when to change a costume and what props are needed for each dance. New dancers can find this nerve wracking, so this list eases their stress and means less questions for me to answer during a show.

Remembering why I started dancing or ever wanted to perform is what motivates me. I write it down and place it in my car or in my touring bag. I usually write on a small piece of paper "to share my story or to inspire others." It doesn't have to be elaborate but a small note to see.

As a young child, I watched dancers perform on a stage and thought it was pure magic how the body could tell a story and make you feel so many emotions without ever saying a word. That's impressive. Asking the dancers why they wanted to do this in the first place can reveal a bit of perspective and clarity on tour. Inspiring others as you dance can transform lives. The audience in front is waiting to absorb the magic dust you are spreading on stage. It is a gift to share stories with thousands of audiences in different cities. With the small amount of time on Earth, dancers realize our bodies can only do this kind of work for so long. For me, it is imperative to share these rare Italian dances with as many people as possible so that they are not lost and forgotten.

After a great performance is done, it is always rewarding to greet fans that come to see you. How to greet the audience is something I think all dancers need to practice as much as possible. Fans will wait to speak with us after the shows and request autographs. We see young children dancing and moving to the beat when we perform. We have inspired them! Even though we are not big stars on Broadway or on television, our work matters and is seen as historical. The dancers are exhausted and dripping with sweat after the show, but it's important to welcome fans with a smile and thank them for coming. They are the reason we are there. I encourage the dancers to practice a brief conversation in front of the mirror.

"Hello, it's nice to meet you, thank you so much for coming today."

"Glad you made it – did you have a favorite piece?"

Engaging in a brief conversation helps build community and offers them a small window into the world of dance. By letting them in, perhaps they might tell others to come to the next show. This is often how communities start to hear about Italian culture and these rare dances we perform.

Since words can carry a great amount of weight, offering to share a bit more after a performance can be an x-factor. You will find the dancers toweling off, sipping a drink of water and pulling themselves together just to say hello. It means more than they think. Audiences usually tell me how they cherished meeting us. Think back to when you saw a great concert or performance. Wouldn't it have meant everything to you if you could have spoken with the performers after the show? Who doesn't want to know more details about the inspiration for a piece or meet your favorite dancer? Our curiosity nudges us to grow.

Each company member knows it's all hands-on deck to make our tour successful. Any extra surge of advertising makes a huge difference in getting the word out. I never understand why dancers work so hard to make the audition and give an excellent performance on stage but tell no one about their show. They should be extremely proud of their hard work and want to shout it from the rooftops every day. I know I feel that way. But since it's my company, it usually all falls on me to spread the word. My list of duties is never-ending.

When I first started the company, we all pitched in to support each other. We attended each other's performances and activities. Using social media has become the norm. However, today, this generation doesn't post too often about their performances. If we don't know when they are then what's the point? Maybe we have bombarded people with too much information? At every rehearsal, dancers would share their upcoming events so we would attend as a unit. I looked forward to their activities. This was part of the bonding experience.

I am finding new ways to curate enthusiasm about cultural dance performances with the next generation so it can gain popularity. Perhaps the yearning for their own heritage is the answer. Like myself, I discovered who I am by learning these dances. So, seeing the performances can be the gateway into seeing their future by learning their past. My speaking engagements usually pique their interests as well. Younger generations have numerous questions that spark a deeper conversation.

By sharing the company's show details, we gain a bigger following. Telling family, friends and neighbors about the next performance can be just enough to drum up excitement in the community. Making these extra efforts and going beyond what is expected for the company goes a long way with me as the director. I recognize those that help. It becomes very noticeable on tour when photos are shared, videos posted, or hashtags go viral. These small acts of initiative create more gigs which means a better investment and a larger population is being educated about these dances! This helps with our preservation project.

Speaking of finances on tour, I have found ways to save while traveling with the company. While there are many costs on tour with costume cleaning, parking, gas money, dancers' fees, and buying new equipment, I factor these types of items in when we have to charge for our performances. We don't have the Medici family budget, but we make every dollar count.

On the flip side, it's crucial for every dancer to have their own checking and savings account set up so they can get paid. Many young dancers might not have this arranged yet. Setting up an automatic savings account allows a dancer to save a portion of their earnings after each show.

By having part of my earnings go straight into a savings account automatically, keeps me from spending it. Even if it is a small percentage, I am saving after each show. By the end of the tour, I see my savings grow. No twenty-something wants to think about retiring or when their dance career might end, but it's important to think about the future. I offer my two cents on finances with them and encourage them to keep saving and keep a close eye on their accounts. I started my dance company at the age of twenty and had to learn financial basics in a short amount of time.

Carpooling, bringing our own food, and offering rehearsals online bring costs down. Over the years, I have welcomed dancers into my own home to stay over if we are in between cities so that they don't have to spend gas money or waste time driving home, especially if they live a far distance. Countless meals have been provided along with rides for dancers that didn't have a car or a way to and from a show. I consider them family where everyone can pitch in to make a difference. No dancer has ever left our group hungry. I strive to demonstrate how a community should always be looking out for one another in various ways.

In the next chapter, you will feel what it's like to perform outdoors in all kinds of weather. I share stories of extreme situations my company has gone through to preserve and present these authentic dances for audiences of all ages.

5,6,7,8

- Do you remember things easily?
- What do you bring on a trip that makes you feel comfortable?
- How do you save money when traveling?
- Why did you start your passion?

Dancing in the rain at a festival.

Dancing Rain Or Shine

Performing at outdoor events such as festivals can be a mixed bag of experiences and problems. Dancing in the open air makes you feel alive and refreshed. When I perform outdoors, I imagine myself in one of the piazzas in Italy. It is an opportunity to bring these beautiful dances to massive crowds that have never experienced it. That's one of the goals, to share the Italian dances with everyone, not just Italian Americans.

People often ask me, "what happens to your show if it rains? Do you still perform?"

The answer is it depends. If the space we are provided has a cover or protection of some kind to keep us safe from a soft rain then yes, the show will go on. But if there is thunder or lightning then it's not safe for anyone including the sound technicians so we postpone or cancel the show. Knock on wood, we haven't canceled too many shows over the three decades of performances. Some venues have a backup building inside where we can move our show easily. That doesn't mean over the years, we haven't weathered a few storms both figuratively and emotionally.

The weather I worry about the most is extreme heat. Dancers can easily get overheated and pass out with heat exhaustion when we are dancing out in the summer sun, without a place of shade to escape to. A few years ago, we were hired to perform for an Italian day celebration at a popular theme park. There were many unknown factors since the park offered vague answers to all my questions. They also didn't seem to have a specific point person in charge of us for this performance. I have a checklist I go through along with a questionnaire the venues fill out before we arrive, but they didn't complete it.

The dancers were so excited to do this particular gig since they were looking forward to riding the roller coasters and having a fun day together as a group. I am not a huge fan of roller coasters since my short, petite body tends to get thrown around in those rides. However, I did see an opportunity for the group to perform, have fun and share these dances with a new audience. So, I booked the gig.

When we arrived, our bags were searched for security which put me at ease. Then, I realized we had a huge walk ahead of us. Oh no...this is pretty far to get to the performance area. My husband and I looked at each other and said, "we need a plan for after the show!" I spotted golf carts that the park workers used to get around.

That's it!

We will tell them we need a cart to transport all our things back to the parking lot. I pulled park personnel aside to relay our plan. As we came around the corner, the park worker gestures and says, "we are here and there is your stage!"

"OH MY" – I said with a scared voice.

This is not going to work at all.

The stage was a small metal area barely ten feet wide that stood about four feet off the ground. It was very rickety and seemed like something I would need a tetanus shot before touching it. I was mortified and frustrated to no end. Just like the dancers, I had higher hopes for this venue. While I was under no illusion that we would be performing in Carnegie Hall, this "stage" was a metal contraption in the middle of the grass patch, while the bleachers and concession stand were well built structures.

I wanted to rip up the contract and leave, but the dancers calmly replied, "Anna, we are going to make it work."

Really?

I always want the best for them. I never want to disappoint them as their leader. I was impressed by their sheer willingness to make the best of this situation. In reality, this was not out of the ordinary. For many venues we perform at, the stage is either too small, insufficiently sturdy or covered in band equipment and endless cords, and we need to make adjustments by performing in a different space in front of the stage or moving equipment and confining our performance to a section. This was another huge life lesson for me that day: do not let your expectations get ahead of reality. Swallowing my pride, I knew we would put on a fantastic show and be grateful for this new opportunity.

My worker bees set up the dressing racks behind the stage and got the props in place in a jiffy. As I was putting on my three layers of costume, my skin began noticing the temperature, since it was close to 94 degrees Fahrenheit. It was an absolutely beautiful day. There were no clouds in the sky.

As I sprayed on sunscreen, my heart picked up speed and my costume was causing me to sweat while getting dressed. I dabbed my face, fixed my makeup and took some deep breaths.

Lord, bring me a cool breeze! At least some of these layers come off during the show!

I could see Greg's face becoming concerned. He brought me over cold water in a bottle to sip on. I set it aside to use throughout the showcase.

Well, it was time. The dancers and I decided to perform on the grassy patch in front of the stage. It was really the only option. Our performance included dances from various regions of Italy along with a swing dance at the end for an upbeat Italian American celebration. The moment I wrapped my fingers around the microphone to do a sound check, I burnt my hand. One of the workers had placed it out in the sun where it sat while we were setting up. I dropped it and scooted it with my foot under the edge of the stage structure where it was shaded and could hopefully cool down before I used it again. I rushed to pour water on my hand. Luckily, it wasn't that bad. I used a towel the next time I picked up the microphone.

Meanwhile, I look around to see where Greg would be running the sound. Next to the audience bleachers, I see a small box-like building where the sound equipment is housed.

This building is air-conditioned! Need I say more?

My husband waves and offers two thumbs up from the cool, clear glass window where he will be watching the show and running our music. I gave him a look of aggravation. Our audience was shaded by beautiful green, leafy trees and not bothered by the heat. Everyone was sitting cool except for me and the dancers.

As my dancers walked to their places, I said with encouragement, "Have a great show everyone! Do your best and if you need breaks, let me know."

My director hat went on and I grew more concerned as the show progressed.

Please God keep us all safe, was my mantra on repeat in my head.

Despite our sweaty bodies, our show was going smoothly. I could see the dancers were expending more energy than usual, and recovery times were lengthening as there was no respite from the sun. Then, the last number was upon us, the swing dance number. Knowing the dance was filled with high energy stunts and difficult choreography with close partner work and tricks, I turned to the dancers and asked,

"Can we do one more dance? Are you all okay?"

Tired, they gave me a yes by nodding their heads, since speaking took too much energy. Reevaluating my own strength and health, I took my place alongside my partner.

The music began and the dancers left every last ounce of energy and drop of sweat on the grassy area that day. We functioned solely on fumes. I still don't know how we made it through. I chalk it up to our training. And that day, I was grateful for my training and all the hard work and late nights the dancers put in. The audience could tell we were giving it everything we had and was applauding loudly with great delight!

Gathering in one line, we took our final bow and went behind the metal stage to change. Like dominoes, dancers began slowly collapsing one after the other. Taking three more steps, I too, slid down to the ground and sat. We were all spent from the heat. The water Greg had given me at the beginning of the performance was hot to the touch. A few of the parents, along with my husband, came behind the metal structure to assist us. We desperately needed to get out of the sun. After a few splashes and sips of water, we carefully changed out of our costumes. Weak and still sweating, I motioned over to the park staff worker for the cart.

Yes – thank goodness for the cart! The dancers' eyes enlarged as they shuffled off to food, water and a shelter to cool down. They changed and made it over to a shelter. Once fed and cooled down, they planned to stay and embrace a few rides to have some fun.

My husband took one look at my flushed face and said, "let's get you home."

I felt as if I was going to faint. My body was overheated and in need of rest and food, *pronto*! On the drive home, Greg debated if he should take me to a hospital. I begged to just go home.

We sacrifice so much for our performances. Our bodies, our strength, and our mental health is pushed to the extremes like any athlete. Sometimes, we give too much. I vowed that day to never return to venues that don't create safe spaces for us to showcase our work. Never again will we accept to perform at a venue that doesn't care about our health and safety. It's not worth it. I needed to be more conscious of requiring shaded areas, as even on beautiful days, there are risks. We are not machines, we are humans. Clearly the park that day didn't realize how bad our situation was. They only cared about entertaining the audience. Thankfully, we all survived, and the dancers enjoyed their time. I benefited from a relaxing bath and dinner.

Mother nature has also challenged us with rain. We have danced in the rain a few times over the years. Nothing too major, just light sprinkles every now and then. Never had to cancel a show.

But there is a first for everything. Isn't there?

Hired to give an Italian dance workshop for an outdoor festival, Greg and I drove about an hour or so to get to this venue. It was just the two of us, no dancers for this gig. On our way there, the rain came and didn't stop. It was coming down so hard we had to pull the car over a few times to see the road ahead. With this much water we wondered if they canceled the festival or postponed it. I wondered if anyone would be there when we arrived.

I was a bundle of nerves the entire car ride. We finally arrived at the festival safely. I got out of the car and saw people walking around with umbrellas and knew it wasn't canceled. Thank goodness for that! As we started to walk towards the festival grounds, the rain subsided from the torrential downpour. Maybe my intense prayers on the way were heard.

I gathered my things from the car and started down a set of stairs to find the point person in charge of entertainment. I spotted him and asked what the plan was since the storm happened. He explained we couldn't do anything outside because of the electrical equipment being a safety hazard. Being the solution slayer that I am, I politely suggested going inside the church building since there were a few vendors inside cooking and selling Italian artwork and gifts. We headed inside the church basement along with others who were walking in that direction to eat and shop.

Once inside the festival worker suggested going ahead and let the audience know you were ready to start the workshop. With a little whistle and a shake of my tambourine, I got the crowd's attention. I announced my dance workshop was about to begin and to grab a friend and join the circle to learn.

In about three minutes flat, twenty-five teenagers and a few adults formed a circle around me.

Wow! My eyes grew large seeing the next generation wanting to learn about their heritage through dance.

Andiamo! Let's go!

The night was filled with fast footwork and lots of twirling as I taught various dances from Italy to the audience. Their faces were sore from smiling and laughing so much. Just a few minutes in, more and more people joined in and by the end of the workshop, three generations were dancing with me. Perhaps the rain was a gift that night.

After they learned a few dances, I treated them to a new solo I was working on to get some feedback. They whistled and cheered loud enough to wake the ancestors of Rome. Many of them were taking videos and photos with their phones and posting fiercely. They were so grateful, and all came up to shower me with kind words after the workshop and performance. This was the first time they experienced these dances and expressed how they would love to do it again.

Yes of course! I replied.

That wasn't the only time the rain changed how or where I danced. The movie *Singing in the Rain* was on repeat in my home as a child. My mom would hum the tune each time it rained. That movie came to mind for this next story.

My dancers were about to perform a beautiful dance called *Saltarello Bolognese* from the Emilia-Romagna region. Performing at an outdoor festival on concrete, unfortunately without any form of shelter, is always challenging and never recommended. The venue did provide us with a small tent where we could change our costumes. Dressed in our northern costumes, each female dancer wore a white, cotton peasant top with a different colored skirt. They had matching aprons filled with pale greens, yellows and a touch of blue and orange flowers that I made. Her waist was cinched with a wide brown belt and her braided hair adorned with faux flowers like a headband. The male dancers wore black pants and a white button-down shirt with a green sash around his waist that was trimmed with gold fringe on the ends. His look was finished with a fedora shaped hat with a colorful feather on the side.

I was especially proud of this costume I pieced together to recreate this look of the 16th century. It wasn't perfect, but it was colorful, elegant and regal, just what we needed. The fabrics for the skirts and shirts were made of a cotton lightweight material to keep the body cool since we dance outdoors often in the summer heat. As the ladies twirled about, the skirt flowed softly creating a gentle movement.

We were getting into our places for the dance, and I looked up and noticed a dark ominous cloud starting to roll in and headed our way. My husband was working the sound for us, happened to glance over at me and we both looked up at the sky with a look of fear. I nodded to him to start the music.

The dance was going well with the dancers walking in time like an army with precision. This dance requires us to make sharp, clean lines using walking steps that go forward and back with a slight curtsy to the partner. We were about halfway through the dance when I felt a drop of rain on my arm. As I shake my partner's arm for a do-si-do move in a Roman handshake by grabbing their forearm, I begin to feel a few more drops of rain trickle across my face. Out of the corner of my eye, I saw the clouds becoming a darker shade of gray. I glanced down the line to all my dancers to see if they were still together. They seemed not to notice the rain drops hitting their bodies.

We get to the last phase of the dance with just about thirty-five seconds to go, when the rain picks up speed and heavier drops are now splashing on us. Umbrellas pop open like fireworks and the audience is starting to huddle around to see us finish. The rain was now taking center stage in our dance performance as if we cued a special effect. As we made our final straight-line formation, I looked at the dancers to see if we needed to stop for our safety. I could start to feel my feet losing grip on the ground and becoming slippery. The dancers shook their heads at me to say, we are not quitting.

Honestly, I was ready to quit. I was afraid of falling and taking the line of dancers down with a ripple effect. As I twirled, I could see water whisking away from the edge of my skirt. I became an instant water slide toy that gets everyone wet as it turns. My entire costume at this point was drenched from head to toe. Thank goodness for my waterproof mascara!

The final chord in the song arrives and the ladies give one more spin and pose. We finished the dance without any injuries, thankfully. I exhaled. The audience erupted into applause. From their point of view, it was a unique showcase of strength, professionalism and a bit of stage effects all rolled into one dance. My mind thought of how Gene Kelly might be proud of our show. I was thrilled the audience didn't walk away the moment it started to rain. Our fans are warriors.

Weather has surely inspired me over the years. It's something I observe each day outside my window. Dancing in the rain that day set my imagination a blaze for a solo using an umbrella as a prop. When I was in Florence, I noticed a woman dancing as a busker in a piazza with an umbrella. Her use of the umbrella so gracefully encouraged me to give it a try. As a young ballerina, I often used a parasol in various shows elegantly, but it wasn't earth-shattering choreography back then.

Desiring to create a solo with the umbrella in an unexpected way, I chose a tango style of movement. The umbrella became my dance partner by holding it in front or by walking around it with the pointed end down on the ground. This challenged the creative process by imagining the prop as my dance partner. The Italian composed song highlighted phrases that tested my footwork and tempo of my gliding moves.

Weather also became a theme for our show a few short years after that rainstorm. I called our tour Stagione meaning season, in Italian. Our opening number was about the different celebrations in Italy according to the season. Some vignettes of movements expressed how holidays were celebrated in Italy. We mentioned *sccopio del carro*, explosion of the cart, from Florence which is a folk tradition around the Easter season. It is a display of fireworks that date back to the first crusades. We also included activities like the horse races in Siena or the Carnevale in Venice. The dancers incorporated movements and props that showcased those events. It was an eclectic piece that captured Italy's four seasons in a snapshot. Innovative choreography brought education to our audience.

As I assemble each touring show, I contemplate what the audience can learn about Italian culture from watching it.

Inside the repertoire that year, was a duet I titled *Seasons of Change* with music by Vivaldi. This idea was on my wish list to experiment with for a long time. Teaming up a ballet dancer with a hip hop dancer performing similar movements side by side, I wanted to express how it feels to be in someone else's shoes. We all have commonalities and in this case our passion for dance. At the end of that duet, the dancers switched roles as the ballet dancer took on hip hop moves and vice versa for the hip hop dancer.

A modern quintet called *Stagione*, named after the theme of our tour, was also presented that year. This dance expressed how we go through seasons in our lives. We all experience storms we never think we will survive or bathe in the sunniest days of celebrations that we hope to go on forever. Then there are seasons of transitions like achievements or goals we haven't reached yet.

For me, transitions in life I portrayed as autumn. The times where we feel like we are in limbo and are just doing our best to make it through each day. Maybe it's your harvest season where you finally see the fruits of your labor from the year.

Spring usually represents a time of rebirth or starting over. A time where you take in a deep breath and feel like you can begin again. A season to feel brave enough to take a leap into a new job or dive deeper into your passion.

Each dancer represented a season: winter, spring, summer and autumn. Working in unison and harmony, the dancers move throughout the space. As a tool for choreography, I had them use the word of the season they represented as the impetus to create a phrase of movement. For example, my word was winter, so I traced out the word using my arms or legs in the space around me. This gave me a chance to experiment with movement and find new ways to express that word.

As each dancer presented their phrase of movement on stage, a fifth dancer who represented change came on the stage and disrupted the flow. The seasons were in a line according to when their season happened. The fifth dancer tried to change the order of the seasons physically. As the choreographer, this moment represents the times we can't avoid or moments in life that knock us out of order. For me, it was the death of loved ones such as my grandparents, my parents and my aunts and uncles. Maybe for others it's finding someone you adore. Each of these moments in life can set us on a different path and create a new order or focal point for our lives. Seasons don't always go as planned. Sometimes, there is a little summer in the middle of our late autumn. This climate change piece taught me to look for the disruptions in life and know that there is always a new way to get back on track.

Resilience is needed to continue to preserve these dances along with the strength of a gladiator to survive touring. In the next chapter you will find my seeds of change along with ways you can preserve heritage and culture.

5,6,7,8

- What season do you feel your best?
- What small action will you take today to get results?
- How can you positively affect someone's life?
- Do you have someone that disturbs your seasons in life?

Dancing a solo for a festival.

Seeds of Change

Throughout my career, I have shared my knowledge through speeches and spoke with thousands of students about the birth of my company and the work it took to get to this point. As I formulated my speeches over the years, I reflected on my grandfather's garden. The main points in my speech are called seeds of change. For me, there are five seeds that have enhanced my growth and improved my life.

The first seed is to do small actions to get big results. Getting to the stage to perform or learning the folk dances straight from Italy are made up of hundreds of small tasks or actions I had to accomplish in order for me to achieve those goals. We make thousands of decisions in our daily lives. I had to make thousands of decisions when I first started my company. My advice is to do small actions every day toward your big goal. Once you have that overarching goal set, work backwards to achieve it. When I wanted to study in Italy, I asked myself what can I do today to achieve this goal?

Traveling adds up to a great deal of money, so I had to make sure to put enough money away each time I got paid to go towards my ventures. Finding the right teachers in Italy also was made up of several small actions that I took.

Asking around, networking with professionals in the field, led me to the right teacher. Doing something small each day adds up and before you know it, you are reaching your target goal. Break your goal down to the smallest of actions, list them all and achieve daily.

The second seed is to build up your skills. Over the years, I have built up a few skills like sewing or how to create a website. These skills were acquired over a length of time, but most of them are free to learn. All of them take practice and time, of course, to navigate properly to put into play. Anything is possible if you are willing to do the work. Sewing is something I work on each time we have a performance. I learn a new feature on my sewing machine or how to hand stitch something in a different pattern. I research every day about a subject I want to know. I usually find a more efficient way to do a task, new vocabulary words or an activity I want to try. Visiting my local library for inspiration, a website or video allows me to try something new. Building up your skills makes you a well-rounded person.

The third seed of change is to change your mindset. Changing your mindset can honestly change your life. I know it's not easy to change your mind nor another person's mind. But for me, I made the decision to remain positive and curious in life. By not having all the answers, I am willing to learn from others. Some of the folk dances are not easy to grasp at first and take a long time to perfect. This can test one's patience. It's easy to become frustrated and discouraged by others. Even when I am doing my best, I can see that others underestimate me and my abilities. Being a woman with her own business, I am bombarded with degrading questions at venues such as asking, where is the director? They assume it should be a man in charge of my group. When I speak up and say I am the director and founder, their faces usually have this shocked look with a bit of embarrassment. Yes, changing your mindset can be difficult if you don't practice each day. My daily goals are written down. Lists have become my road map to survival. Some days, I achieve all the items and other days I don't. But this practice helps me remain positive knowing I am on the right path.

The fourth seed is to affect or change one person's life today, then you can change the world. I believe in the butterfly effect. The notion that helping one person will in turn help others. Now that my company has been around for thirty years, I see how I have greatly affected each dancer's life. Some dancers met because of Allegro, found love, got married and now have children that dance and enjoy traditional Italian culture with their growing family. Other dancers made lifelong friendships that have helped them endure difficult times in their life like a big move, a job loss, or a death in their family.

Taking a chance in creating an Italian touring dance company based on my college thesis project was a leap of faith. I had no idea how it would work, how far we would travel or how long it would last. As time passed, experience and perspective were abundant, it was clear to me with each decision I made for my company, it influenced each dancer and the lives of their future families. Kind gestures, such as passing on advice about an upcoming audition or writing a recommendation letter for them to receive a scholarship in college, paved a way for their success. Caring for the next generation with these actions gave students a guide on how to create opportunities for others.

Changing one person's life in turn changes a community. It's in my blood to help others. My parents demonstrated endlessly how to volunteer in the community, assist with church functions or raise money for people in need. Each time I visit Italy, complete strangers are always kind enough to offer directions or assist me to have a clear understanding. My grandparents would serve food to anyone that walked through their door. Sharing a piece of their lives meant they cared for your well-being. The moment our hands meet when we gather in our circles to dance our traditions, we begin that sharing of open hearts and coming together as one. Kind acts are never too small to make a difference.

The last seed is to physically plant a seed, water and watch it grow. This might seem simple, but it is the one activity that has helped me visualize my own growth. Planting a seed teaches us to be patient with ourselves and understand that growth happens each day even if we don't see it. As a child, I would plant a seed in a cup and each day I would examine it to look for any changes. By giving it water and sunlight, I noticed a difference. I, too, was growing alongside it. Seeing my growth alongside the plant, created a greater awareness of how things change.

As a child, this was magical and thrilling. Perhaps, it still is as an adult. Life is always evolving and changing, like my dances. My enthusiasm for gardening has grown over the years. I look forward to seeing the seeds bloom into fragrant basil, juicy tomatoes or sweet peppers. Planting something gives us purpose. It prepares us to be patient for all things to become beautiful. I guess waiting is the hardest part. The best part may be the fact you can share what you have grown with those around you. This is what I admire about finding the dances in Italy. I now get to share them with everyone. Witnessing others delight in what you have grown brings more joy than anyone will ever understand.

Words of wisdom still echo from my mentors as I make decisions in life. Sometimes saying thank you to a teacher or mentor is not enough for the endless inspiration and encouragement they give you. Since I am a huge fan of thank you cards, I enjoy buying and sending them out to those that made a difference in my life. I often mail a thank you card to festivals or organizations where we have performed as a gesture of gratitude. Over the years, I have cherished many of the cards I have received from dancers, students, and performance venues. A person smiles a bit brighter when receiving appreciation in written form. When someone thinks of me enough to take time out of their schedule to let me know I made a difference to them, they motivate me to keep going. My cards are curated in a box with other special notes and letters. From time to time, I shuffle through and reread them. This particular card I came across caught my eye.

It read:

Anna, thank you so much for all the work you have put into choreographing this show. It looks so great thanks to you! I admire the skill you possess and all your patience with the less experienced dancers such as myself. I have always appreciated your bubbly personality and the energy you bring to every rehearsal. You also have a great sense of humor! At first, I was intimidated by your no-nonsense attitude during the last rehearsal. However, that is when I really started to see progress in myself and in others. This has been one of the best experiences I have had. You really do know your stuff and I'm never going to doubt your methods again.

This student was in a musical for a community theater I choreographed. Moved as I read through this again, I didn't realize I impacted her so deeply. As a teacher, I continuously toss my thoughtful seeds and hope for a great harvest season. Making someone feel confident and giving them the tools needed to perform well is astonishing to watch. Their growth each time they take the stage is like watching your garden grow. When the lights go up and you hear the applause, that's when you see your seeds come to life and bloom. The knowledge, work, and insights you gave them took root and are flourishing in front of you.

My students have become a second family to me. Family means everything in Italian culture. We go to great lengths to find and be with our family. We sacrifice parts of our lives to take care of each other. When I was a little girl, my father would bring me to visit him at work from time to time. When he introduced me to others, he would say this is my daughter, the dancer. My eyes would light up and look up at him when he said dancer. While I was thrilled and adored that he called me a dancer, the more important title was daughter. Being his daughter meant I was family and I belonged. Family is a strong word for me. I define it as the people around a table sharing a meal, holding hands praying at church, or moving in time dancing. Family wants to cheer and celebrate my achievements, as well as be supportive when everything fails.

People often ask a child what they want to be when they grow up. With confidence, I always said a dancer. There has never been a doubt in my mind. Without any regrets, I made that dream come true, but now I realized why. Why did I want to be a dancer? Answering the question of why gave my life meaning and a path to my truth.

I became a dancer because I wanted to serve and to give back to my community. I dance to honor my ancestors that gave me a heritage and history to protect, to preserve, and celebrate. Dance provides a means to deliver joy to people, teach cultural history, and share stories of life lessons. This was my gift from God. My grandparents told me to treasure my gift and share it with the world. Dance is my breath and prayer. Honoring these dances from Italy is a chance to preserve traditions and history for the next generations that have yet to discover them.

If I don't share these dances, I fear they will disappear. Now that my grandparents, parents and all aunts and uncles have now departed, I see traditions and cultural dances rapidly disappearing before my eyes. I am realizing I am a future ancestor and want future generations to enjoy these dances. I urge everyone to talk about heritage with family, especially children and grandchildren. Share more than how to make that one special dish. Teach them about being an active family, participate in the traditions, the holidays and the everyday activities that make the culture so special and interesting. For me, dance offered a way to communicate thoughts, prayers or emotions. Italian dance was my treasure chest filled with stories, music, and ways to love. I finally held the key to unlock and explore.

There are numerous ways to help preserve these cultural dances. Create opportunities where communities can have an open dialogue about the traditional dances to foster more knowledge. Try an Italian dance class or create a performance opportunity where community members can show off their new dance skills. Make sure your library has books about Italian dance so that future generations can learn.

Every time I am met with closed doors, I search for an open window to share these dances. If preservation isn't done, these pieces of our heritage will disappear, and the future generations will have no knowledge that they ever existed. It's an important part of Italian culture that needs a light shined on it. So I am turning on every light and taking every opportunity I come across to showcase, demonstrate and preserve these works of art.

Contact a local educational institute and start a conversation about offering cultural dance and music classes often. Offering courses to local schools or universities is another great way for younger generations to be immersed in the culture with these authentic dances. I have taught numerous workshops for schools and universities in person and online. Each time we finish a workshop, the reaction is the same. WOW, why didn't I do this earlier? This is where the next generation can start to witness living history and obtain the knowledge to share with the next generation and so on.

The arts encapsulate our traditions and life lessons within them, which are necessary to preserve our heritage. I gained an immense amount of life skills from learning these dances. From looking someone in the eye to being a good partner or being able to switch directions quickly. These skills allow me to thrive in life and make better decisions.

It's time to make plans and hold a dinner and dance party night. Spread some good vibes by moving with those you love. Dancing is good for the mind, body, and spirit, but it's also good for our community. So gather your family and friends and try something new, even if you have two left feet, everyone will feel the joy from these elegant dances. It's not how well you do the dance steps but the act of learning them and sharing them is what counts. By doing these dances, you share in the history, the heritage and the legacy of those ancestors.

The dances of northern Italy are where I found power, wealth, and innovations. Movement is powerful and discovering my heritage through researching these dances, not only brought an endless wealth of knowledge, but also the innovative solutions. These solutions came from the process of seeking these dances which opened me up to the creativity that was hidden inside. Studying dances from northern Italy brought me an unusual key to great happiness. With every door that was met, I found a key to unlock it and discover more to share and preserve. I am ready to share my key with the world. Are you ready to open the door?

The key to success, to happiness, to love, lives in each of us because *bellezza nun trova porte chiuse*, beauty does not find closed doors. Be beautiful, be brave and unlock the door to your traditions by dancing!

5,6,7,8

- What is your gift? How do you intend to share it?
- What kind of impact are you making in your community?
- Who do you consider as family?
- How do you plan on preserving your traditions?

Acknowledgments

Thank you to my quest readers for sharing your thoughts and great feedback. You make writing exciting and fun to share.

I want to share my deepest gratitude to my mentors, and instructors that danced beside me to make sure I was getting the steps correctly. Your patience and guidance allow me to bring out the true beauty in these dances.

To my family and friends in Italy: You allow me to bring the past, present and future together. Leading me to the answers that I was seeking and sharing a wealth of history that brought me joy. Showing me kindness every step of the quest. Thank you for being an example of what it means to be a community of love.

About the Author

Anna Pishner Harsh is the Artistic Director and founder of Allegro Dance Company. Anna's grandparents made a home when they came to the United States in the early 1920's from Reggio di Calabria, Italy. She holds a M.A. degree in Communication from West Virginia University and a B.A. degree in Dance from Slippery Rock University. She is also a certified Pilates and RYT200 Yoga instructor. Through her extensive research in Italy over the years with various teachers, she continues to grow her repertoire of authentic Italian dances to share with audiences of all ages. These precious dances hold history, express various emotions and are sacred and ceremonial.

Her determination to preserve traditional Italian dances is seen. Her creative and sunny disposition is found in her writing and choreography. Her never-ending passion for dance along with her Italian heritage is boundless. Anna and her husband Greg enjoy traveling and researching together. Read more about Anna's travels, her family heritage and the start of her company in her first book, *La Danza, Conflict, Passion, and Healing.*

Join our circle

Welcome to the dance circle!
Learn these dances and keep moving!
For classes, speaking engagements, and newsletters Visit www.AnnaHarsh.com

Listen to Anna's podcast called
THE DANCE FLOOR PODCAST
Where life lessons are learned through the art of dance.

Read more about Anna's Italian dance preservation with her first book:
La Danza – Conflict, Passion, and Healing

If you loved this book, please tell others and write a positive review!

www.ingramcontent.com/pod-product-compliance
Ingram Content Group UK Ltd.
Pitfield, Milton Keynes, MK11 3LW, UK
UKHW021649190726
13853UKWH00001B/154